لغتنا الجميلة

Name : ....

Level : ....

Author: Mona Elnahrawy

Reviewed By: Yehia Youssef

اعداد : مني النحراوي

مراجعة : أ. يحيي يوسف

Note to Teachers and Parents

This publication is a part of a comprehensive series designed to teach Arabic as a secondary language. It is devised to establish a firm core for Arabic, especially for reading and writing introductory words. The Arabic alphabet is instructed to the students in a letter-by-letter approach. Each letter has its corresponding noun that assists the student to reminisce about the alphabet. Through successful trials, upon completion of the publication, students were able to recognize letters and the corresponding noun to the letter. The rigorous curriculum in this textbook exceedingly keeps students interested, learning, and having fun throughout the duration of Arabic class. Upon successful completion of the textbook, students will be able to decipher the Arabic alphabet with ease. This textbook's specific functionality is **for class use only**. All types of educational institutions require work outside the classroom; parents are highly advised to follow up with their student's progress in order to see exceptional results. The combined efforts of the parents, teachers and the hard work of the students will pay off at the end of the curriculum. Good luck on your journey throughout this curriculum, and as with all other activities, practice makes perfect!

Best Wishes,

**Note from the Author:

I started putting this book together from my experience teaching kids Arabic at various weekend schools here in the United States. I was on a curriculum advising committee of many weekend schools and have used great curriculums. I analyzed what motivated children whose Arabic wasn't their first language to learn Arabic and what kept them from reading or forgetting the material. I put all the missing skills that I have observed from my students in a series of Arabic books intended to make them read within the shortest time possible. I kept in mind that most of the students only had time during the weekend to learn, so I designed the Arabic series to give as much material as possible that is effective during this time. Also, I considered the fact that our classes are melting pots, these series of books are written for everyone, and the books have shown the same effect on students with different backgrounds. My goal out of it is to help kids read Arabic and speak it. I hope this book brings joy to teachers, parents and student.

Sincerely,

Mona Elnahrawy

حروف الهجاء

ث	ت	ب	أ
ج	ح	خ	د
ذ	ر	ز	س
ش	ص	ض	ط
ظ	ع	غ	ف
ق	ك	ل	م
ن	و	هـ	ي

حرف الألف

أ

أ

أرنب

Ar-Nab

أرنب

Ar-Nab

Trace over the dots:

ألوان
Alwan

Trace over the dots:

أ	أ	أ	أ	أ	أ
أ	أ	أ	أ	أ	أ
أ	أ	أ	أ	أ	أ
أ	أ	أ	أ	أ	أ
أ	أ	أ	أ	أ	أ

أسد

Asad

Trace over the dots:

أ	أ	أ	أ	أ	أ
أ	أ	أ	أ	أ	أ
أ	أ	أ	أ	أ	أ
أ	أ	أ	أ	أ	أ
أ	أ	أ	أ	أ	أ

أناناس
Ananas

Write letter (أ) in each box

لون المربعات التي تحتوي على الحرف (أ)
Color the boxes that have the letter (أ)

ضع دائرة حول حرف (الألف) (أ)

Put a circle around the letter (أ):

مفتــاح   بـاب   أســد

صل الكلمات التي تبدأ بالحرف (أ) :

Match the letter (أ) to the word that start with it:

أرنب

تمساح

أسد

بطة

لون الحرف (أ)   Color The letter (أ)

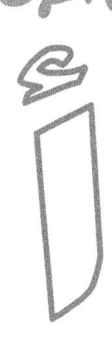  

حرف الباء

باب

Bab

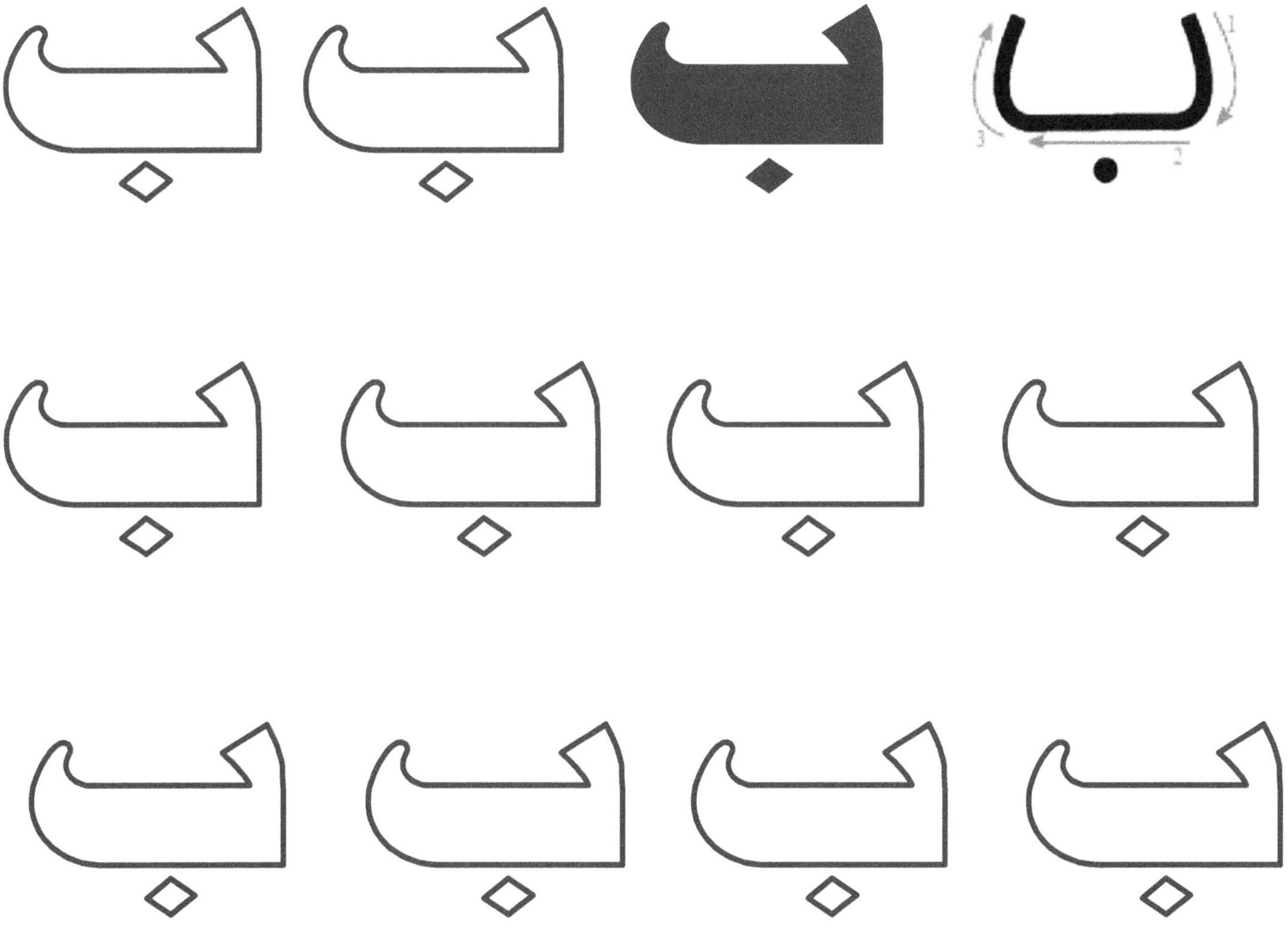

باب

Bab

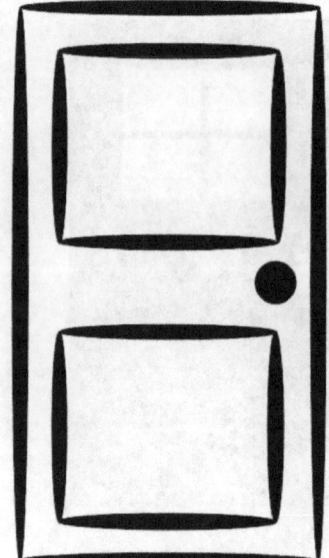

Trace over the dots:

بطة

Bata

Trace over the dots:

بيت

Bayt

Trace over the dots:

بنت
Bent

<u>Write letter (ب) in each box:</u>

لون المربعات التي تحتوي على الحرف (ب):
Color the boxes that have the letter (ب):

ضع دائرة حول حرف (الباء) (ب):
Put a circle around letter (ب):

حبل   بطة   حليب

صل الكلمات التي تبدأ بالحرف (ب):
Match the letter (ب) to the word that start with it:

لون الحرف (ب):   Color The letter (ب):

  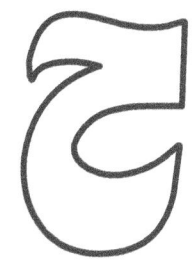

حرف التاء

تمساح
Temsah

تمساح
Temsah

Trace over the dots:

تفاح
Tophah

Trace over the dots:

تاج

Tag

Trace over the dots:

توت

Tot

Write letter (ت) in each box:

لون المربعات التي تحتوي على الحرف (ت)

Color the boxes that have the letter (ت):

ضع دائرة حول حرف (التاء) (ت):

Put a circle around the letter (ت):

صل الكلمات التي تبدأ بالحرف (ت):

Match the letter (ت) to the word that start with it:

لون الحرف (ت) :   Color The letter (ت):

حرف الثاء

ثعلب
Thalab

ثعلب

Thalab

Trace over the dots:

ثعبان
Thoaban

Trace over the dots:

ثور

Thowr

Trace over the dots:

ثوب
Thowb

Write letter (ث) in each box:

لون المربعات التي تحتوي على الحرف (ث):
Color the boxes that have the letter (ث):

ضع دائرة حول حرف (الثاء) (ث):

Put a circle around the letter (ث):

مثلث   كمثرى   ثعلب

صل الكلمات التي تبدأ بالحرف (ت):

Match the letter (ث) to the word that start with it:

لون الحرف (ث) :   Color The letter (ث):

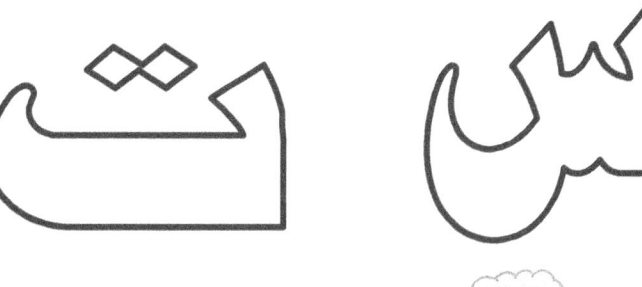

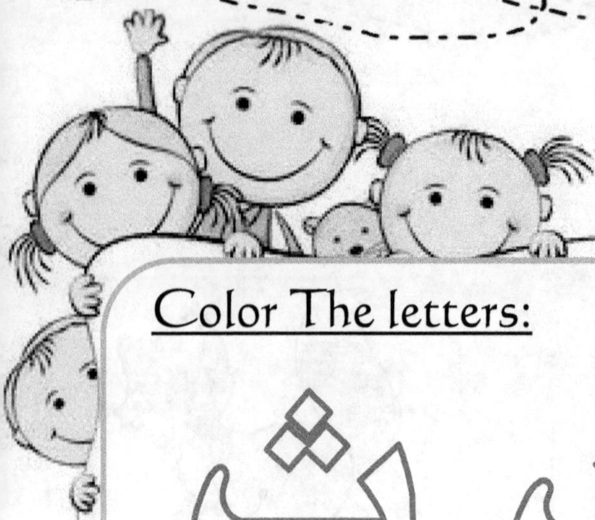

Color The letters:

لون الحروف :

أ ب ت ث

Write the letter that the picture begins with:

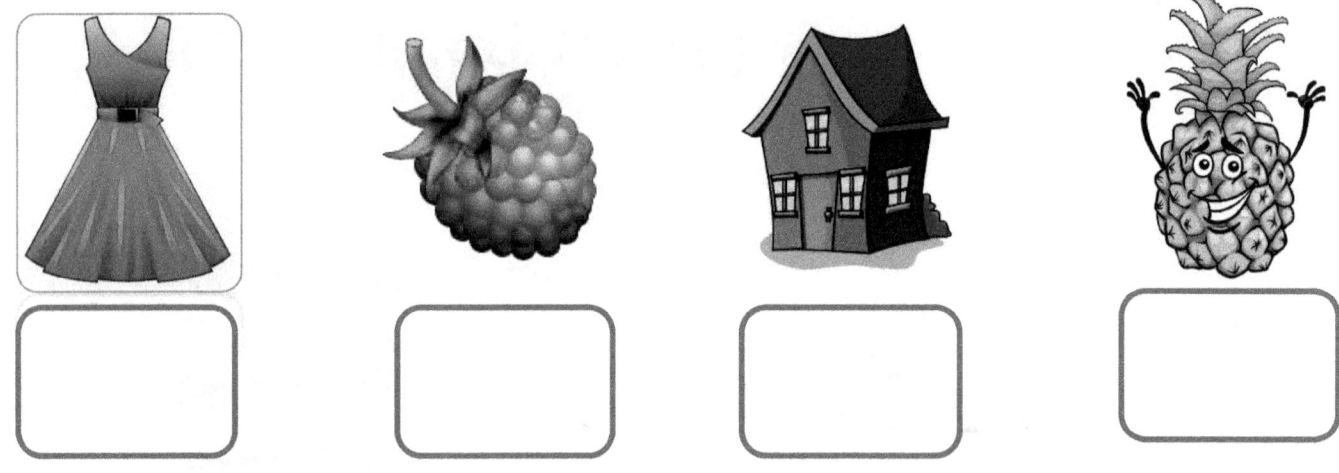

لون الحرف الصحيح الذي تبدأ به الكلمات الآتية:

Colour in the circle with the correct letter that each word starts with:

ثور

ث ب

تمساح

أ ت

بنت

ب ث

أرنب

ت أ

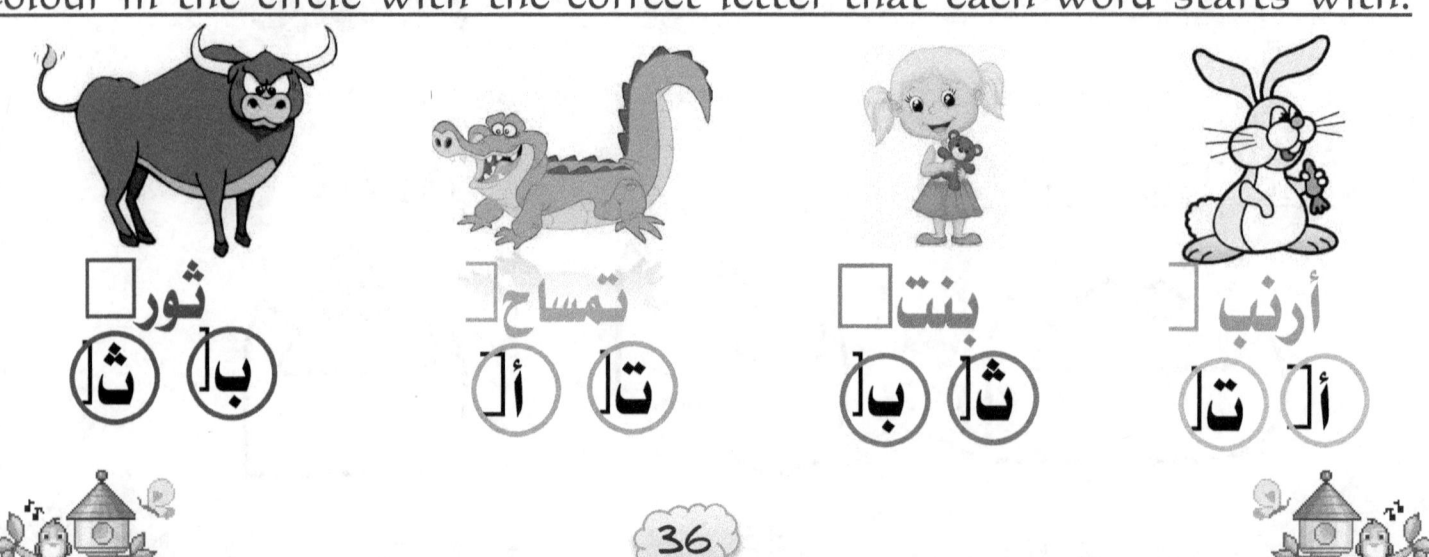

حرف الجيم

جمل

Jamal

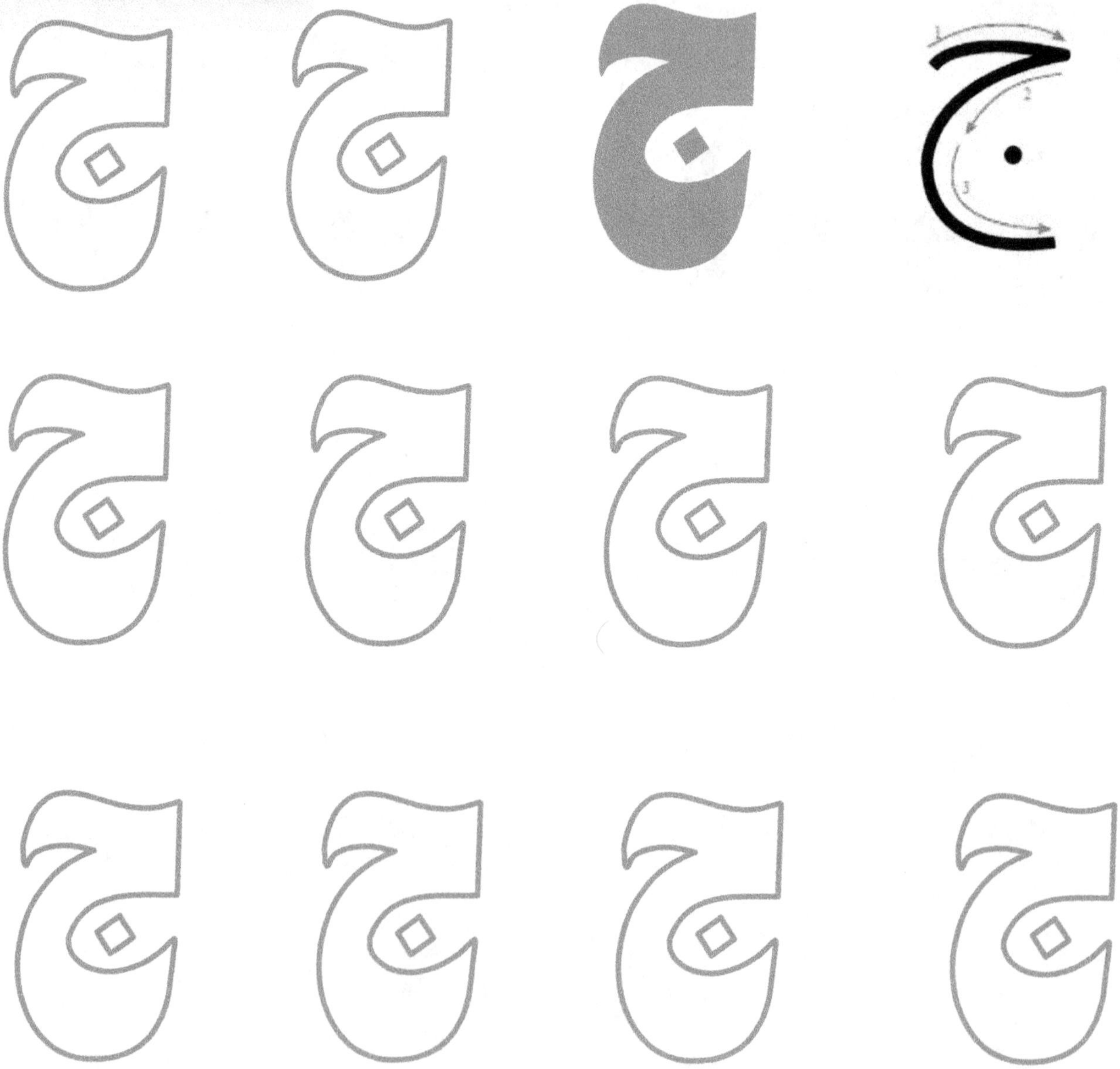

ج

جمل
Jamal

Trace over the dots:

جزر
Jazar

Trace over the dots:

جرس
Jaras

Trace over the dots:

جبن

Jebn

Write letter (ج) in each box:

لون المربعات التي تحتوي على الحرف (ج):
Color the boxes that have the letter (ج):

ضع دائرة حول حرف (الجيم) (ج)
Put a circle around the letter (ج):

دجاجة   فنجان   جمل

- - - - - - - - - -

صل الكلمات التي تبدأ بالحرف (ج):
Match the letter (ج) to the word that start with it:

دجاجة
ثعبان
جزر
جسر

- - - - - - - - - -

لون الحرف (ج):   Color the letter (ج):

س   ج   د

حرف الحاء

حمامة

Hamamah

ح

حمامة
Hamamah

Trace over the dots:

حصان
Heesan

Trace over the dots:

Hakeba

Trace over the dots:

حلوى
Halwa

Write letter (ح) in each box:

لون المربعات التي تحتوي على الحرف (ح):
Color the boxes that have the letter (ح):

ضع دائرة حول حرف (الحاء) (ح):
Put a circle around the letter (ح):

حمامة   لحم   بلح

صل الكلمات التي تبدأ بالحرف (ح):
Match the letter (ح) to the word that start with it:

حصان
تفاح
حلوى
أسد

لون الحرف (ح):
Color the letter (ج):

حرف الخاء

خروف

Kharoof

خ

خروف
Kharoof

<u>Trace over the dots:</u>

خيار
Khyaar

Trace over the dots:

خوخ
Khokh

Trace over the dots:

خيمة
Khayma

Write letter (خ) in each box:

لون المربعات التي تحتوي على الحرف (خ):
Color the boxes that have the letter (خ):

ضع دائرة حول حرف (الخاء) (خ):

Put a circle around the letter (خ):

خروف   نخلة   كوخ

- - - - - - - - - - - - - - - -

صل الكلمات التي تبدأ بالحرف (خ):

Match the letter (خ) to the word that start with it:

خيار
حمامة
تمساح
نخلة

- - - - - - - - - - - - - - - -

لون الحرف (خ):   Color The letter (خ):

Color The letters :   لون الحروف :

Write the letter that the picture begins with:

لون الحرف الصحيح الذي تبدأ به الكلمات الآتية

Colour in the circle with the correct letter that each word starts with:

حرف الدال

دولاب
Dolaab

د

دولاب
Dolaab

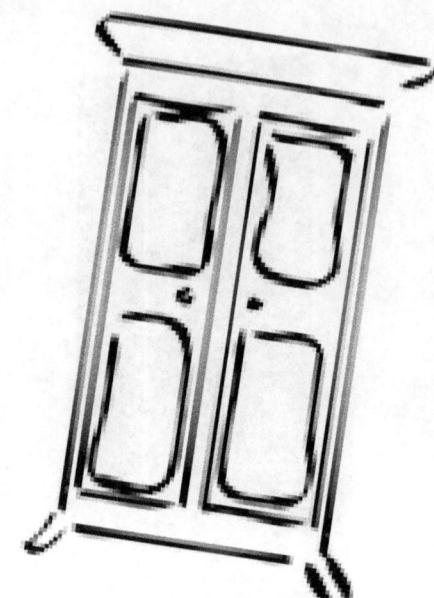

Trace over the dots:

دب
Dob

Trace over the dots:

دراجة
Daragaa

Trace over the dots:

ديك
Deek

Write letter (د) in each box:

لون المربعات التي تحتوي على الحرف (د):
Color the boxes that have the letter (د):

ضع دائرة حول حرف (الدال) (د):
Put a circle around the letter (د):

دراجة   قرد   دودة

صل الكلمات التي تبدأ بالحرف (د):
Match the letter (د) to the word that start with it:

- دجاجة
- حصان
- ثعبان
- بطة

لون الحرف (د) :
Color The letter (د):

  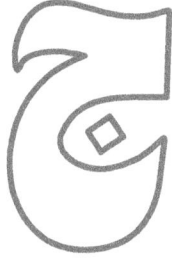

حرف الذال

ذرة
Thora

Trace over the dots:

ذئب

Theab

Trace over the dots:

ذراع
Theraa

Write letter (ذ) in each box:

لون المربعات التي تحتوي على الحرف (ذ)
Color the boxes that have the letter (ذ)

ضع دائرة حول حرف (الذال) (ذ) :

Put a circle around the letter (ذ):

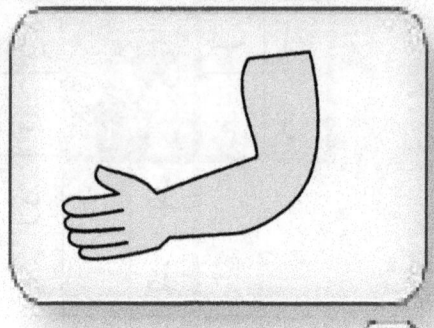  

ذراع   باذنجان   ذباب

صل الكلمات التي تبدأ بالحرف (ذ) :

Match the letter (ذ) to the word that start with it:

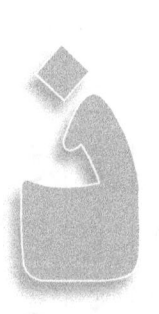

- ذئب
- دولاب
- ذراع
- حلوى

Color the letter (ذ):   لون الحرف (ذ) :

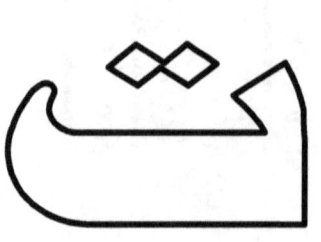

76

حرف الراء

رمان

Roman

ر

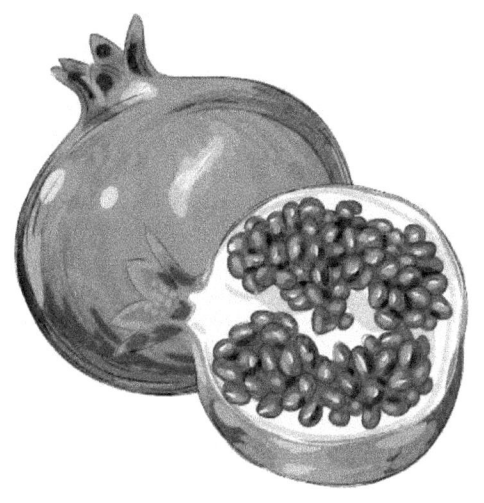

رمان
Roman

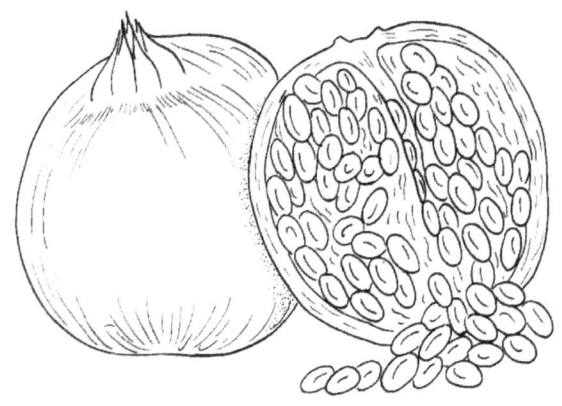

Trace over the dots:

ريشة
Resha

Trace over the dots:

رمح
Remh

Trace over the dots:

راديو
Radio

Write letter (ر) in each box:

لون المربعات التي تحتوي على الحرف (ر):
Color the boxes that have the letter (ر):

ضع دائرة حول حرف (الراء) (ر)

Put a circle around the letter (ر):

برج   قرد   رمح

صل الكلمات التي تبدأ بالحرف (ر):

Match the letter (ر) to the word that start with it:

رجل
دولاب
ريشة
أناناس

لون الحرف (ر):   Color the letter (ر):

حرف الزين

حرف الزين

زرافة

Zarafa

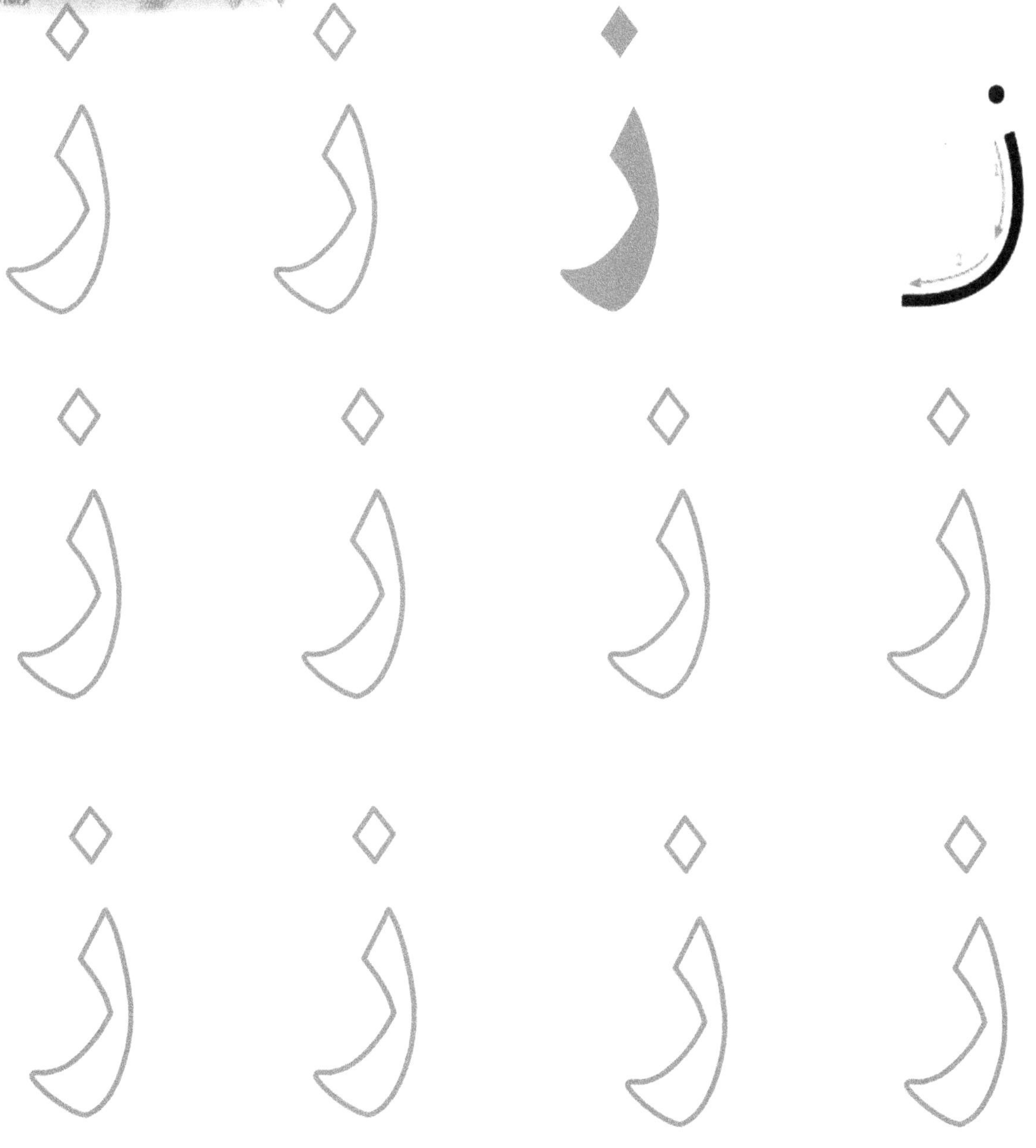

ز

87

زرافة
Zarafa

Trace over the dots:

زهرة
Zahra

Trace over the dots:

زجاجة
Zogaga

Write letter (ز) in each box:

لون المربعات التي تحتوي على الحرف (ز):
Color the boxes that have the letter (ز):

ضع دائرة حول حرف (الزين) (ز) :

Put a circle around the letter (ز):

غزالة □   خبز   زرافة

صل الكلمات التي تبدأ بالحرف (ز) :

Match the letter (ز) to the word that start with it:

لون الحرف (ز) :   Color the letter (ز):

Color The letters:
لون الحروف :

ر ر ذ د

Write the letter that the picture begins with:

اكتب الحروف الناقصة في المكان المناسب:
Fill in the missing letters in their proper spots

حرف السين

سمكة

Samaka

س س س ڛ

س س س س

س س س س

سمكة

Samaka

Trace over the dots:

سيارة
Sayara

Trace over the dots:

سفينة

Safena

Trace over the dots:

ساعة

Saeaa

Write letter (س) in each box:

لون المربعات التي تحتوي على الحرف (س):
Color the boxes that have the letter (س):

		ظ	ن	ل	ع	ج	ه	و	ج	ن	د	ش	ي	ذ	خ
		ظ	م	م	ض	ز	ف	ز	ض	د	ح	ع	خ	ح	د
		و	ز	ن	م	ا	ك	ج	ح	ف	د	ش	ي	ذ	خ
ث	ن	ز	ن	ذ	خ	ت	ث	ت	م	ل	ا	غ	ع	خ	ح	د	ن	ث
ذ	ج	ذ	ي	ذ	ز	ن	و	ط	س	و	س	س	ز	س	س	س	س	ج	ذ
		س	س	ي	ذ	ج	ه	س	ج	س	س	ي	س	س	ب	س	س
		س	س	س	ز	ك	ن	ج	ح	س	س	س	س	س	س	س	س
		س	س	ت	ذ	ج	ح	س	س	س	س	س	س	س	س	س	س
		س	س	س	د	ك	م	ز	س	س	غ	ع	ف	ق	ث	ص
		س	س	س	س	س	س	س	س	س	غ	ف	ز	ف	ز	ر
ث	ت	س	س	س	س	س	س	س	س	س	د	س	ا	ك	ا	ب	ك	ت	ث
ي	د	ز	ي	ر	د	ك	م	ز	د	خ	غ	ع	ف	ق	ث	ص	د	ي
			ز	ي	ر	د	ك	م	ز	د	خ	غ	ع	ف	ق	ث	ص
			ز	ي	ر	د	ك	م	ز	د	خ	غ	ع	ف	ق	ث	ص
			ز	ي	ر	د	ك	م	ز	د	خ	غ	ع	ف	ق	ث	ص

ضع دائرة حول حرف (السين) (س):
Put a circle around the letter (س):

فأس   سمكة   لسان

صل الكلمات التي تبدأ بالحرف (س):
Match the letter (س) to the word that start with it:

ساعة
زرافة
سيارة
ذراع

لون الحرف (ج): Color the letter (ج):

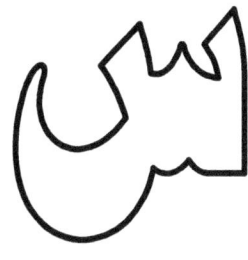
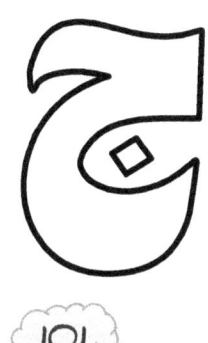

حرف الشين

ش

شمس
Shams

ش ش ش ش

ش ش ش ش

ش ش ش ش

شمس

Shams

Trace over the dots:

شجرة
Shagara

Trace over the dots:

شمسية
Shamsya

Trace over the dots:

شباك
Shibak

Write letter (ش) in each box:

لون المربعات التي تحتوي على الحرف (ش):
Color the boxes that have the letter (ش):

ضع دائرة حول حرف (الشين) (ش):
Put a circle around the letter (ش):

مشمش ☐   عش ☐   شمسية

- -

صل الكلمات التي تبدأ بالحرف (ش):
Match the letter (ش) to the word that start with it:

- -

لون الحرف (ش):   Color the letter (ش):

حرف الصاد

ص

صقر
Saker

ص ص **ص** ص

ص ص ص ص

ص ص ص ص

صقر
Saker

Trace over the dots:

صاروخ
Sarokh

Trace over the dots:

صندوق

Sondok

Trace over the dots:

صفارة
Sofara

Write letter (ص) in each box:

لون المربعات التي تحتوي على الحرف (ص)
Color the boxes that have the letter (ص)

ضع دائرة حول حرف (الصاد) (ص):
Put a circle around the letter (ص):

مقص   صقر   بصل

صل الكلمات التي تبدأ بالحرف (ص):
Match the letter (ص) to the word that start with it:

ص

- صفارة
- شجرة
- حمامة
- صندوق

لون الحرف (ص):   Color the letter (ص):

حرف الضاد

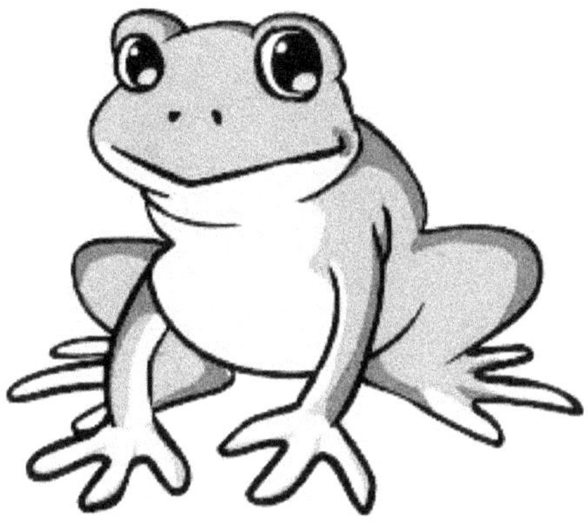

ض

ضفدع
Dofdaa

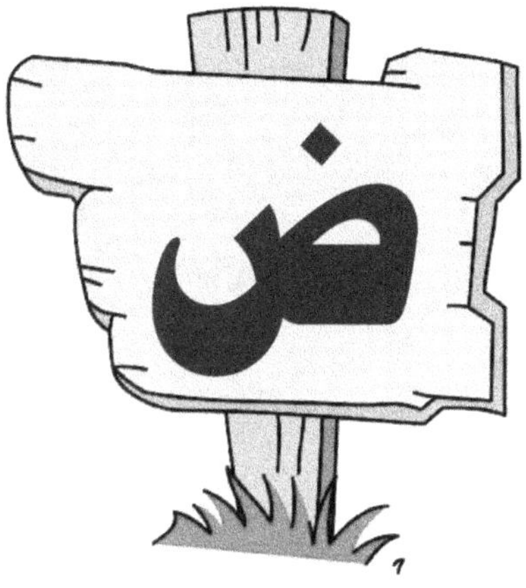

ض ض ض

ض ض ض

ض ض ض

ضفدع
Dofdaa

Trace over the dots:

ضبع
Dabaa

Trace over the dots:

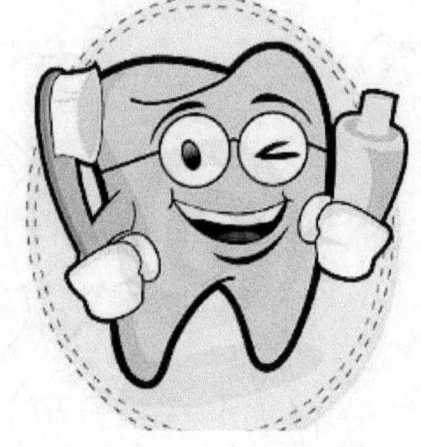

ضرس

Derss

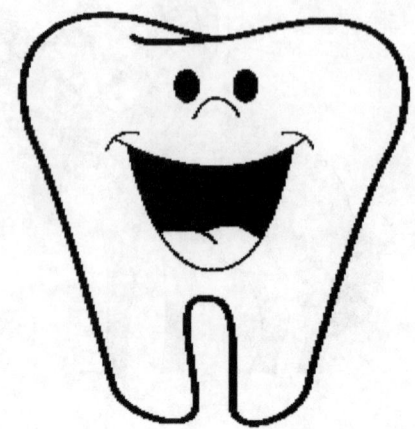

Trace over the dots:

ضابط
Dabet

<u>Write letter (ض) in each box:</u>

لون المربعات التي تحتوي على الحرف (ض):
Color the boxes that have the letter (ض):

ضع دائرة حول حرف (الضاد) (ض)

Put a circle around the letter (ض):

صل الكلمات التي تبدأ بالحرف (ض):

Match the letter (ض) to the word that start with it:

لون الحرف (ض):

Color the letter (ض):

Color the letters: | لون الحروف :

Write the letter that the picture begins with:

اكتب الحروف الناقصة في المكان المناسب:

Fill in the missing letters in their proper spots

حرف الطاء

طائرة
Ta-eh-ra

طائرة
Ta-eh-ra

Trace over the dots:

طماطم
Tamatem

Trace over the dots:

طبلة

Tabla

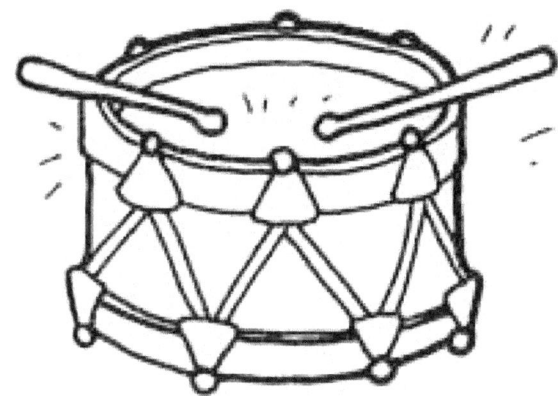

Trace over the dots:

طبيب

Tabeb

Write letter (ط) in each box:

لون المربعات التي تحتوي على الحرف (ط):
Color the boxes that have the letter (ط):

ضع دائرة حول حرف (الطاء) (ط):
Put a circle around the letter (ط):

طبلة   بطة   وطواط

- - - - - - - - - - - - - - - - - - -

صل الكلمات التي تبدأ بالحرف (ط):
Match the letter (ط) to the word that start with it:

باب
طائرة
شمسية
طبيب

- - - - - - - - - - - - - - - - - - -

لون الحرف (ج):   Color the letter (ج):

134

حرف الظاء

ظرف

Zarf

Trace over the dots:

ظبي

Zabi

Trace over the dots:

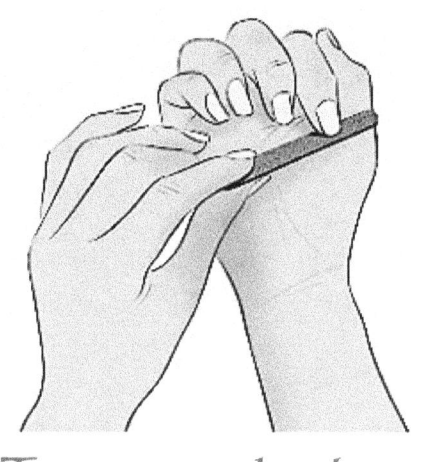

ظفر

Zofr

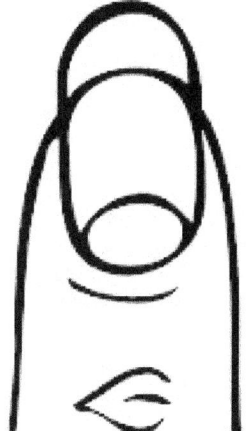

Trace over the dots:

ظل
Zell

Write letter (ظ) in each box:

لون المربعات التي تحتوي على الحرف (ظ):
Color the boxes that have the letter (ظ):

ضع دائرة حول حرف (الظاء) (ظ):

Put a circle around the letter (ظ):

صل الكلمات التي تبدأ بالحرف (ظ):

Match the letter (ظ) to the word that start with it:

لون الحرف (ظ):

Color the letter (ظ):

حرف العين

عصفور
As-foor

ع

عصفور
As-foor

Trace over the dots:

عنب
Aenab

Trace over the dots:

   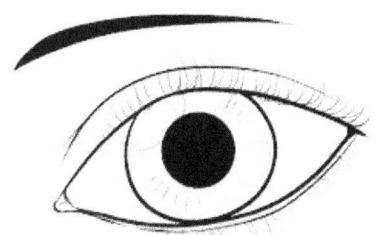

Ayyn

Trace over the dots:

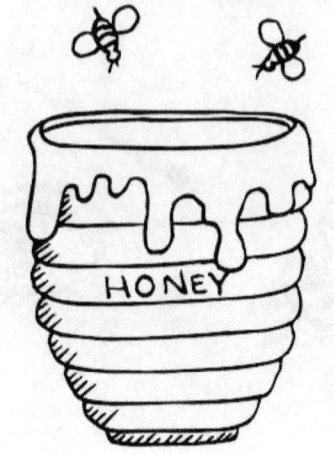

عسل

Assal

<u>Write letter (ع) in each box:</u>

لون المربعات التى تحتوى على الحرف (ع):

Color the boxes that have the letter (ع):

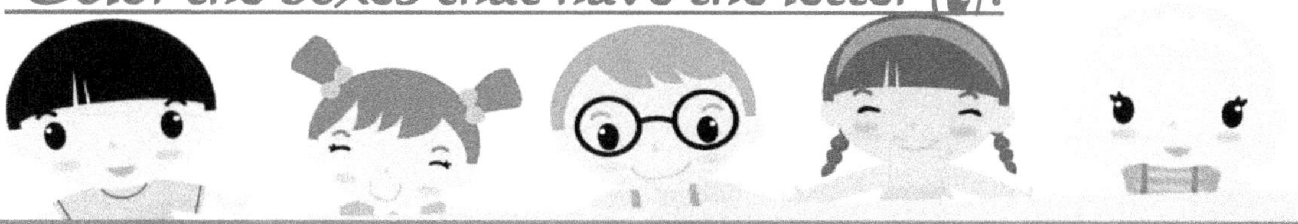

ش	د	د	ف	خ	ك	ل	ظ	ظ	ظ	ب	ي	ر	د	ش	د	ذ
ض	ح	ح	غ	د	ح	م	ظ	ظ	ظ	ر	ط	د	ر	ز	د	د
ظ	ب	ر	ر	ز	م	ه	م	ن	ن	ك	م	ذ	د	ظ	ز	و
				خ	م	ع	ع	ع	ن	ك	م	ه				
				ش	د	ع	ع	ع	ع	أ	ل	ه				
				د	غ	ب	ر	ع	ع	ج	خ	ط				
				ح	غ	ف	ه	ع	ع	ك	ق	م				
				ص	ل	ع	ع	ع	ف	خ	ح	ج				
				ص	ظ	ع	ع	ع	ع	ع	ث	ج				
				ه	م	ل	ظ	ظ	ظ	ع	ع	ر				
				ث	ق	م	ظ	ظ	ظ	ع	ع	د				
				ن	ن	ك	ق	أ	ل	ع	ع	ه				
				ف	ح	خ	ق	د	ز	ع	ع	د				
				ز	ح	خ	ظ	خ	د	ع	ع	ذ				
				خ	ع	ع	ع	ع	ع	ع	ع	ه				
				ف	ع	ع	ع	ع	ع	أ	ل	ى				
ف	ح	خ	ظ	د	غ	ف	ه	و	ن	ك	ق	م	ن	ز	ظ	د
ي	ف	ف	ت	ح	ل	ت	ع	غ	ف	خ	ح	ج	د	ذ	ظ	و
ج	خ	خ	ض	ف	ظ	ت	د	ذ	ر	ض	ث	ج	و	ز	ظ	د

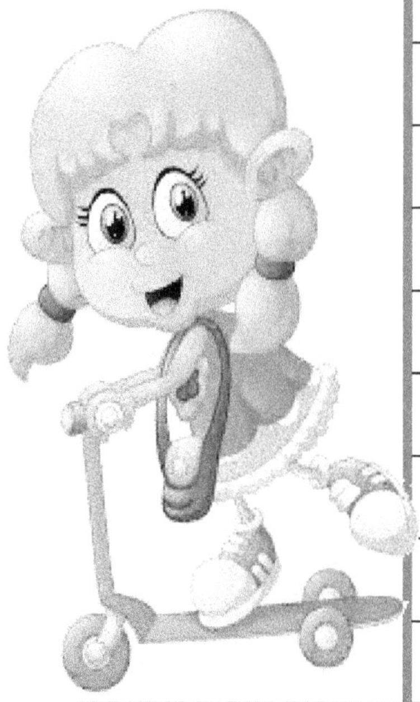

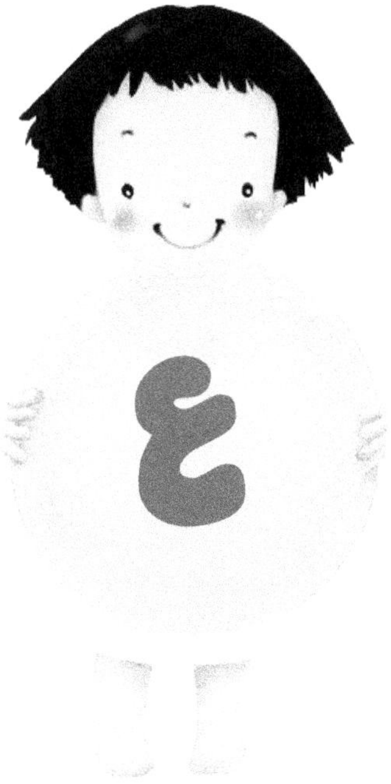

ضع دائرة حول حرف (العين) (ع)

Put a circle around the letter (ع):

ساعة   عنب   ملعقة

صل الكلمات التي تبدأ بالحرف (ع):

Match the letter (ع) to the word that start with it:

لون الحرف (ع):   Color the letter (ع):

حرف الغين

غراب

Ghou-raab

 غ

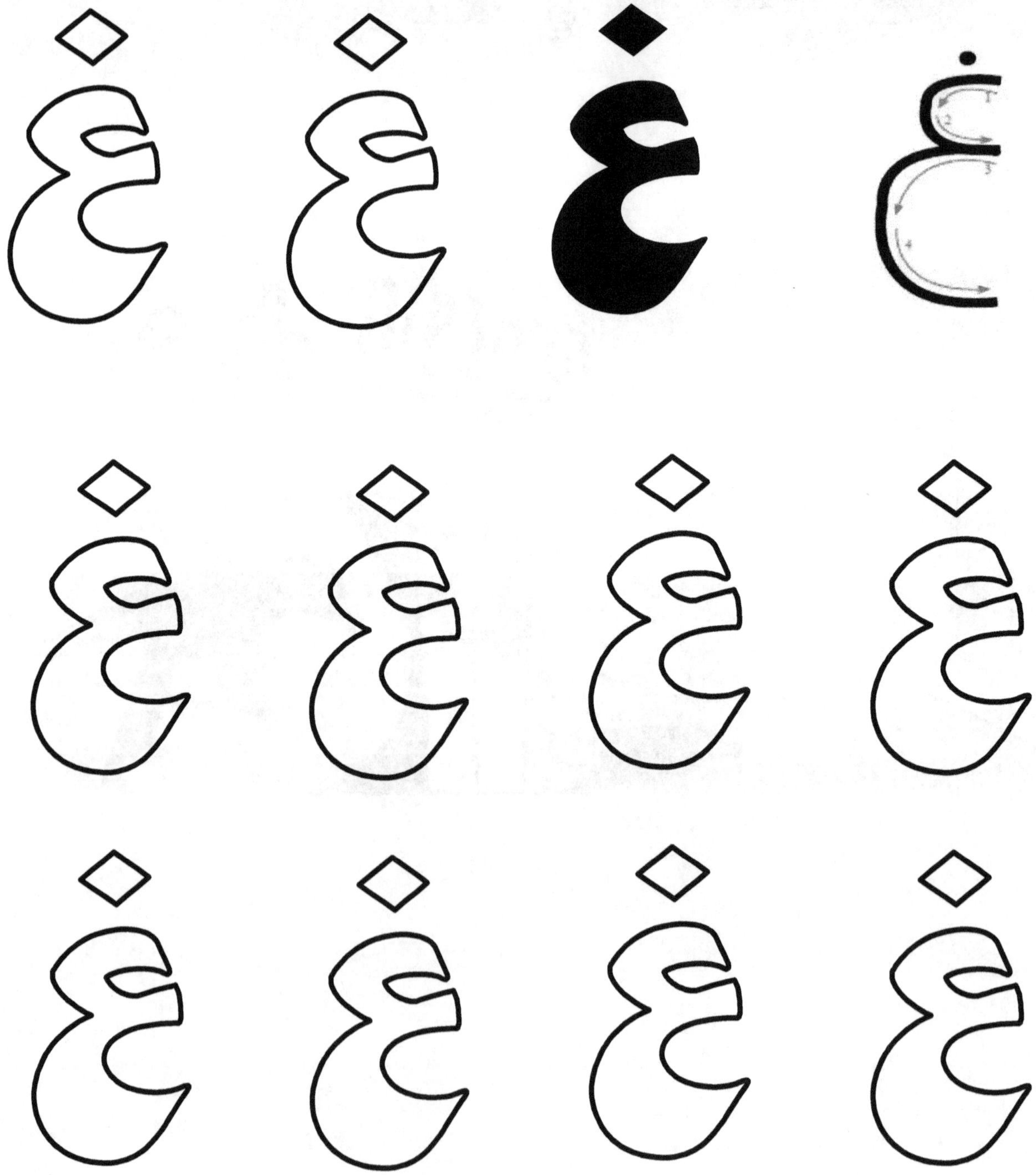

غراب
Ghou-raab

Trace over the dots:

غواصة
Ghawasa

Trace over the dots:

غ	غ	غ	غ	غ	غ
غ	غ	غ	غ	غ	غ
غ	غ	غ	غ	غ	غ
غ	غ	غ	غ	غ	غ
غ	غ	غ	غ	غ	غ

غزال
Ghazaal

Trace over the dots:

غوريلا
Ghorella

Write letter (غ) in each box:

لون المربعات التي تحتوي على الحرف (غ):

Color the boxes that have the letter (غ):

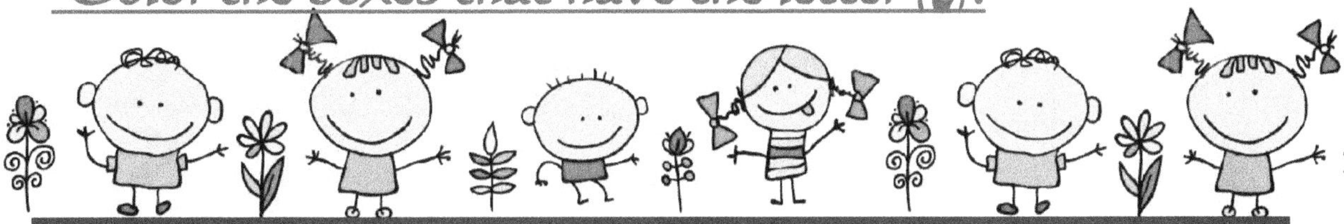

ش	ص	ض	ع	ظ	ت	د	ذ	ر	ض	ث	ج	و	ز	ظ	ج	د
ب	ر	ر	ز	ذ	ب	ف	ه	و	ن	ع	ذ	د	ظ	ز	ع	و
ح	خ	ظ	ع	غ	ف	غ	و	ن	ك	ق	م	ن	ز	ظ	ش	د
ب	ث	ت	ع	ل	ل	ل	ل	ف	خ	ح	ج	د	ذ	ظ	ي	و
ش	ص	ض	ع	ظ	غ	غ	غ	ر	ض	ث	ج	و	ز	ظ	ج	د
			ع	ك	غ	غ	غ	غ	ب	ي	ر	د	ش			
			ع	ح	م	ظ	غ	غ	ر	ط	د	ر	ز			
			ع	ح	غ	غ	غ	ل	ل	و	ف	ه	و			
			ف	ع	غ	غ	غ	غ	غ	ك	د	ر	ي			
			ز	ذ	ع	ك	ف	غ	غ	غ	ذ	د	ظ			
			ع	ك	ف	ل	ت	ن	غ	غ	غ	ن	ز			
			ع	ل	ت	ظ	ت	ف	خ	غ	غ	ن	ذ			
			ع	ظ	ت	د	ذ	ر	ض	غ	غ	و	ز			
			ع	ك	ل	ظ	ظ	ظ	ب	غ	غ	د	ش			
			ع	ح	م	ظ	ظ	غ	غ	غ	د	ر	ز			
ح	ج	ج	ع	ح	ع	م	أ	غ	غ	ع	ع	ع	ع	ع	ز	ع
ص	ث	ق	غ	غ	غ	غ	غ	غ	غ	ك	د	ر	ي	ز	ي	د
ب	ر	ر	غ	غ	غ	غ	غ	غ	غ	غ	ذ	د	ظ	ز	ع	و
ح	خ	ظ	ع	غ	ف	ه	و	ن	ك	ق	م	ن	ز	ظ	ش	د
ب	ث	ت	ع	ل	ت	ع	ن	ف	خ	ح	ج	د	ذ	ظ	ي	و

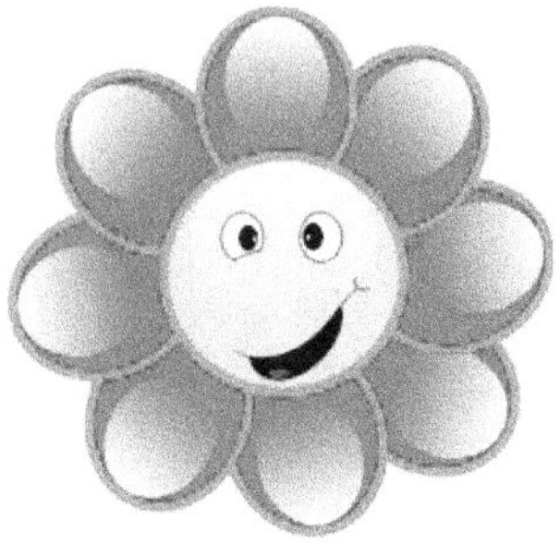

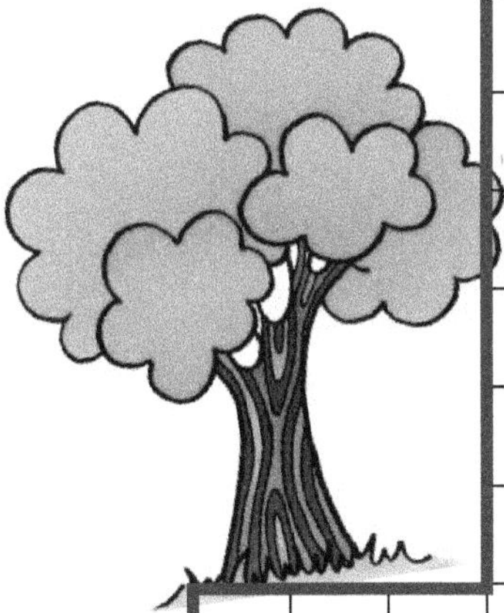

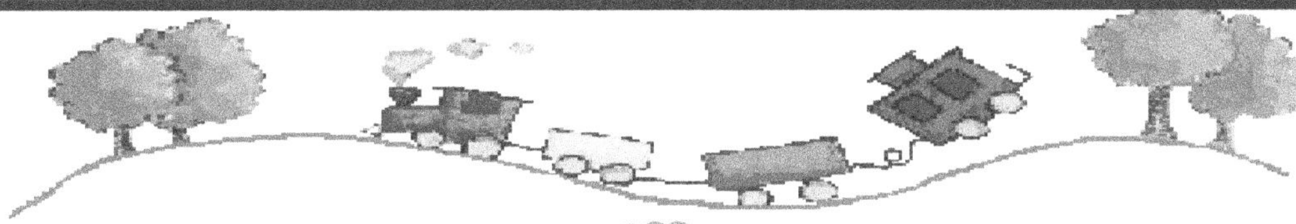

ضع دائرة حول حرف (الغين) (غ):
Put a circle around the letter (غ):

غراب   صمغ   غزال

صل الكلمات التي تبدأ بالحرف (غ):
Match the letter (غ) to the word that start with it:

غروب

عين

غوريلا

أناناس

لون الحرف (غ):   Color the letter (غ):

Color The letters :   لون الحروف :

ط   ظ   ع   غ

Write the letter that the picture begins with:

لون الحرف الصحيح الذي تبدأ به الكلمات الآتية

Colour in the circle with the correct letter that each word starts with:

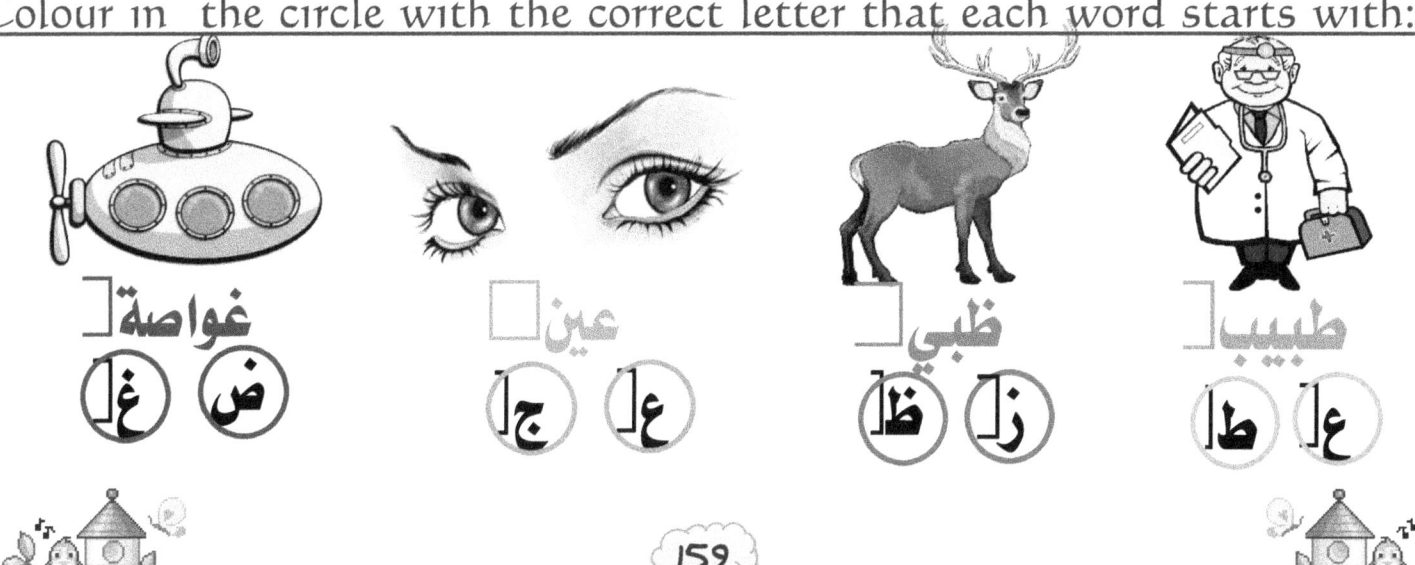

حرف الفاء

فراشة
Farasha

ف

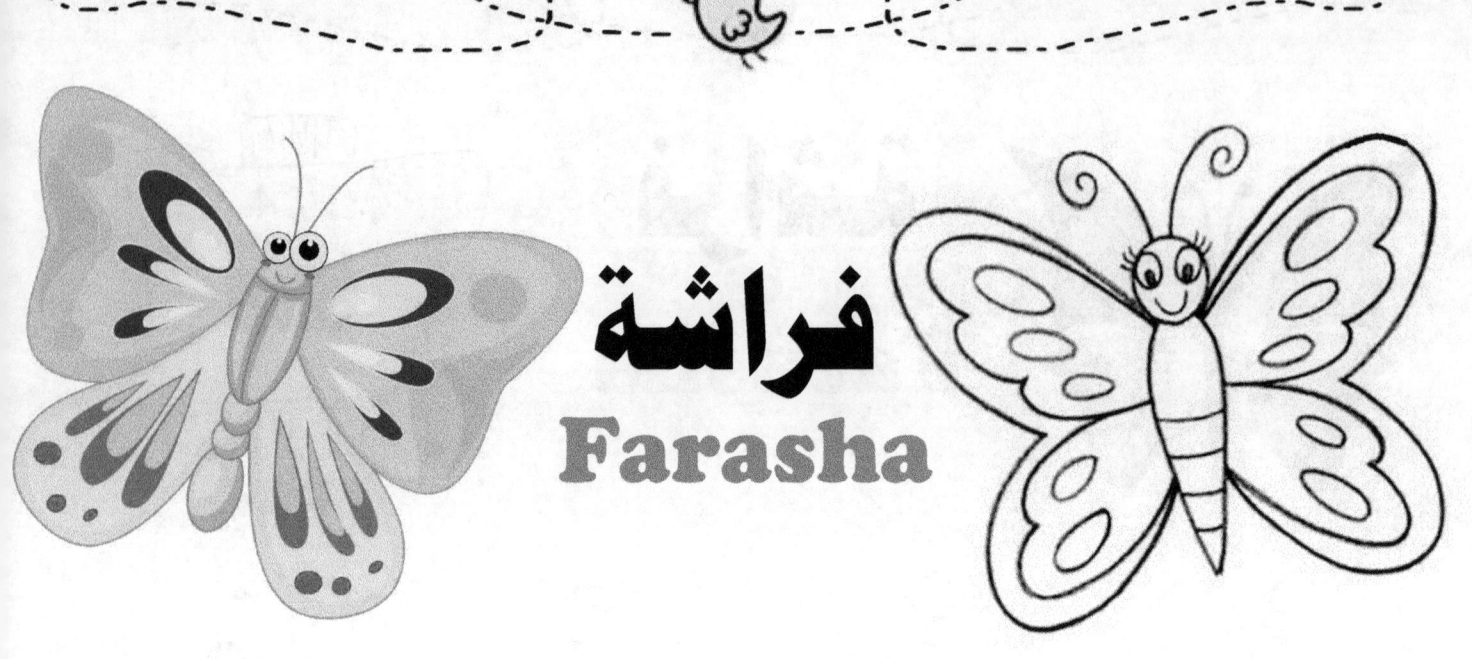

فراشة
Farasha

Trace over the dots:

فيل

Feel

Trace over the dots:

فراولة
Farawla

Trace over the dots:

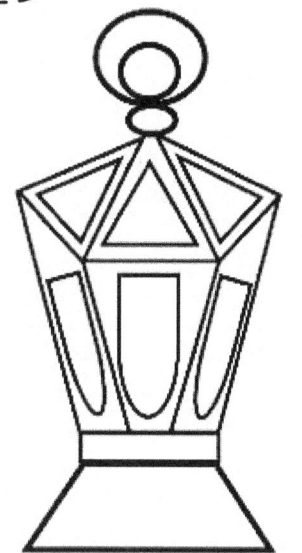

فانوس
Fanoos

Write letter (ف) in each box:

لون المربعات التي تحتوي على الحرف (ف):

Color the boxes that have the letter (ف):

ضع دائرة حول حرف (الفاء) (ف):

Put a circle around the letter (ف):

فراولة   قفل   فأر

صل الكلمات التي تبدأ بالحرف (ف):

Match the letter (ف) to the word that start with it:

دولاب
حصان
فراولة
فيل

لون الحرف (ف):

Color the letter (ف):

حرف القاف

قلم

Qalam

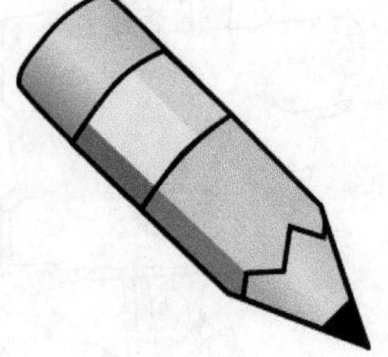 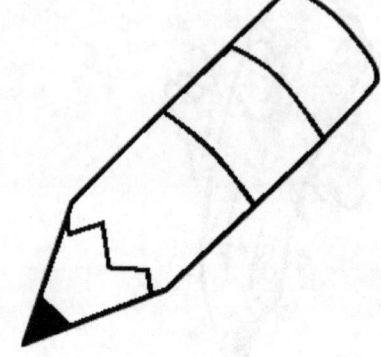

قلم
Qalam

Trace over the dots:

قلعة
Qalaa

Trace over the dots:

قارب
Qareb

Trace over the dots:

قرد

Qerd

Write letter (ق) in each box:

لون المربعات التي تحتوي على الحرف (ق):
Color the boxes that have the letter (ق):

ضع دائرة حول حرف (القاف) (ق):
Put a circle around the letter (ق):

بقرة   مقص   قلم

صل الكلمات التي تبدأ بالحرف (ق):
Match the letter (ق) to the word that start with it:

باب
قرد
سيارة
قلم

لون الحرف (ق):   Color the letter (ق):

حرف الكاف

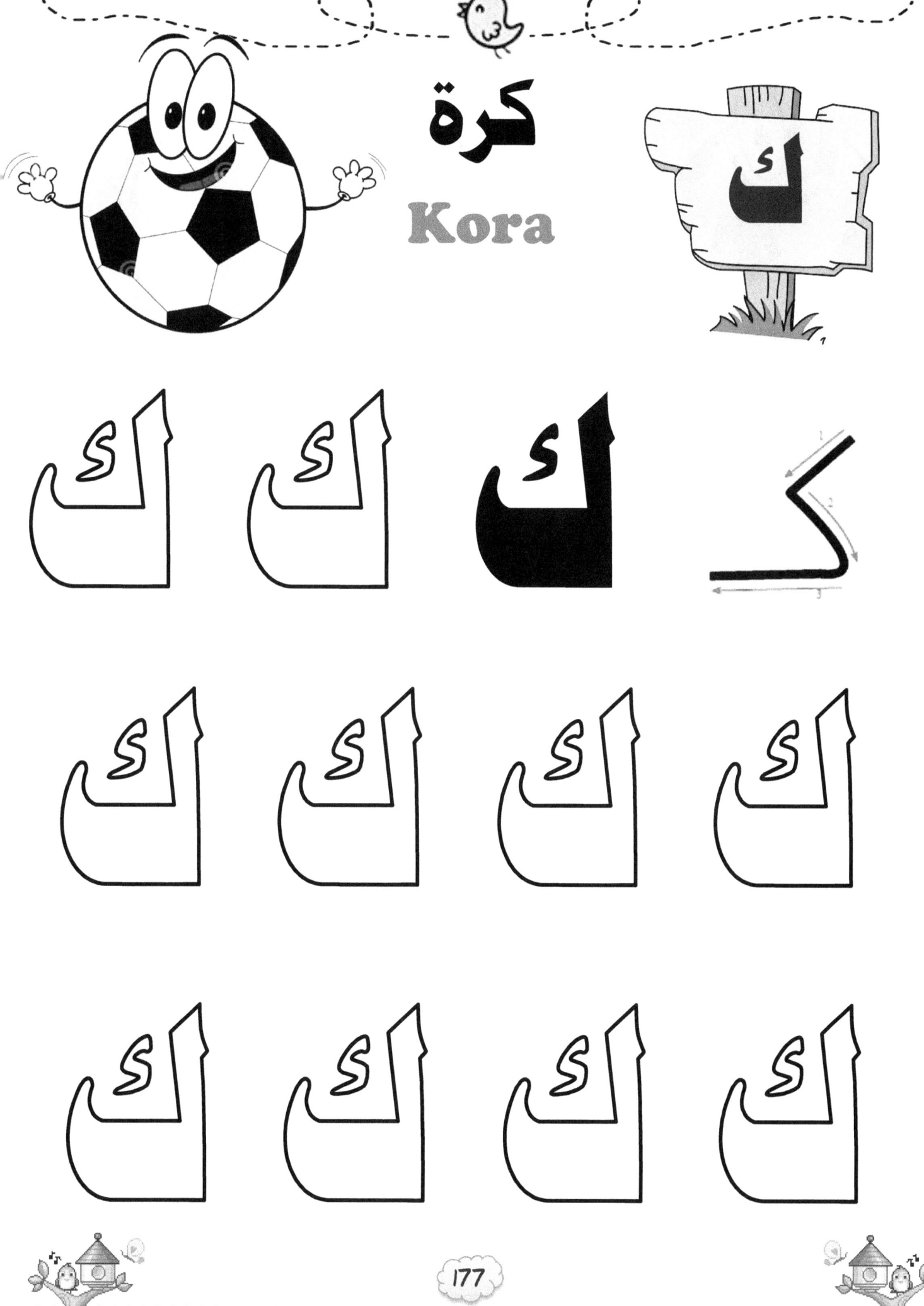

كرة
Kora

Trace over the dots:

كأس

Kaas

Trace over the dots:

كلب

Kalb

Trace over the dots:

كرسي
Korsi

Write letter (ك) in each box:

لون المربعات التي تحتوي على الحرف (ك):
Color the boxes that have the letter (ك):

ضع دائرة حول حرف (الكاف) (ك):
Put a circle around the letter (ك):

كتاب   سمكة   عنكبوت

صل الكلمات التي تبدأ بالحرف (ك):
Match the letter (ك) to the word that start with it:

كأس
فراشة
كتاب
طاولة

لون الحرف (ك):   Color the letter (ك):

ك   ظ   ص

183

حرف اللام

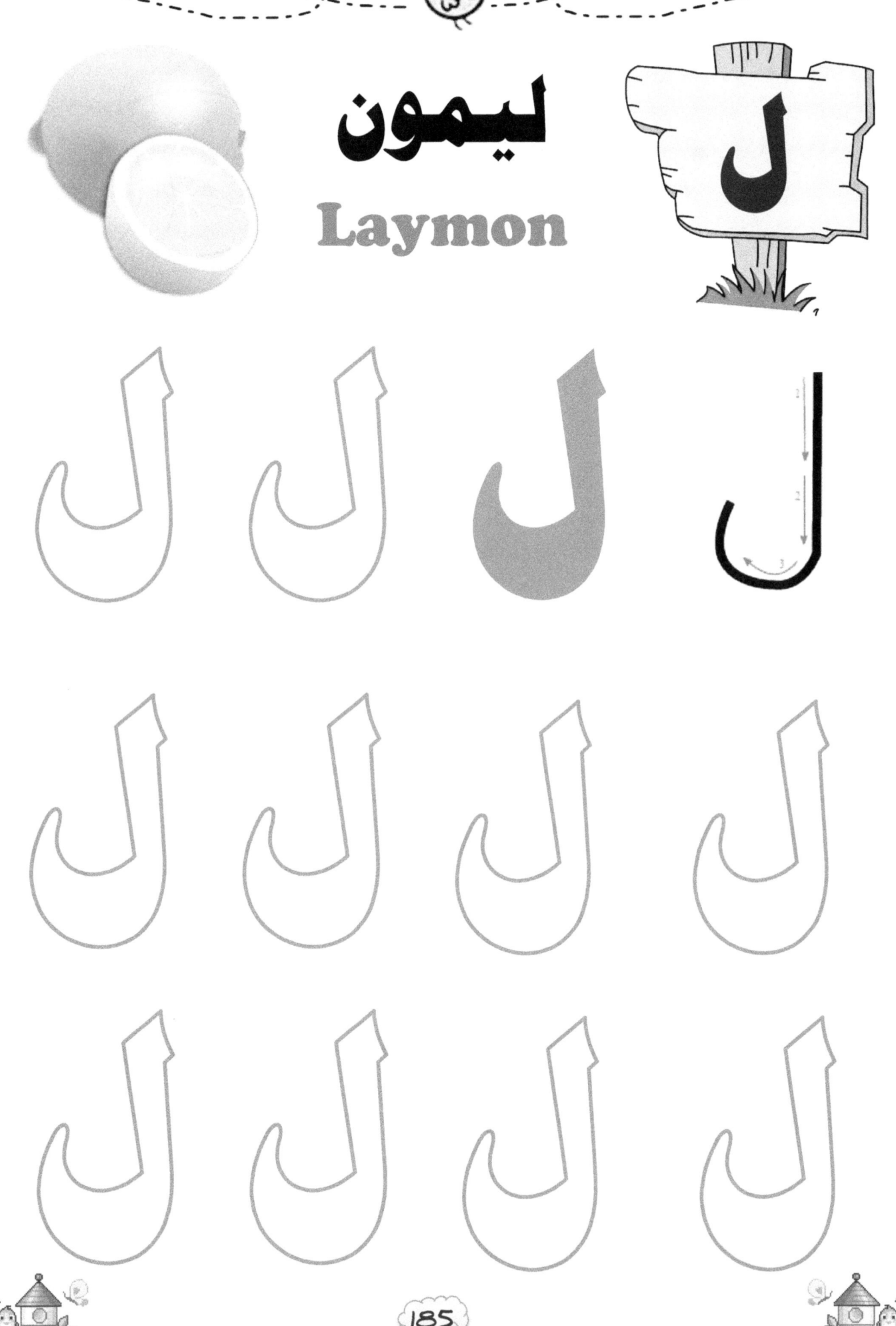

ليمون

Laymon

Trace over the dots:

Lamba

Trace over the dots:

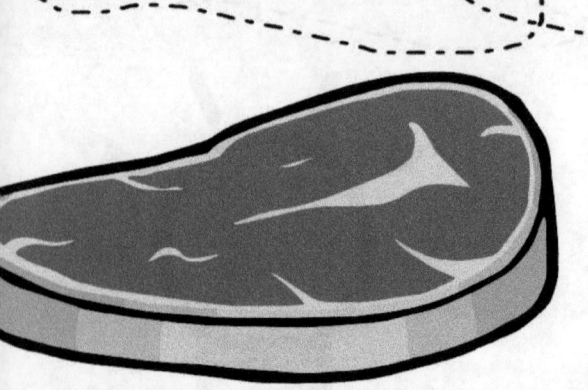

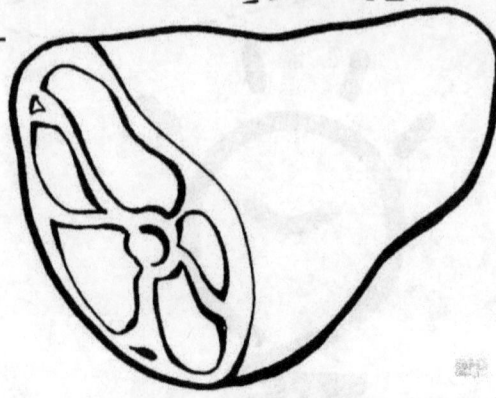

Lahem

Trace over the dots:

لسان
Lesan

Write letter (ل) in each box:

لون المربعات التي تحتوي على الحرف (ل):

Color the boxes that have the letter(ل):

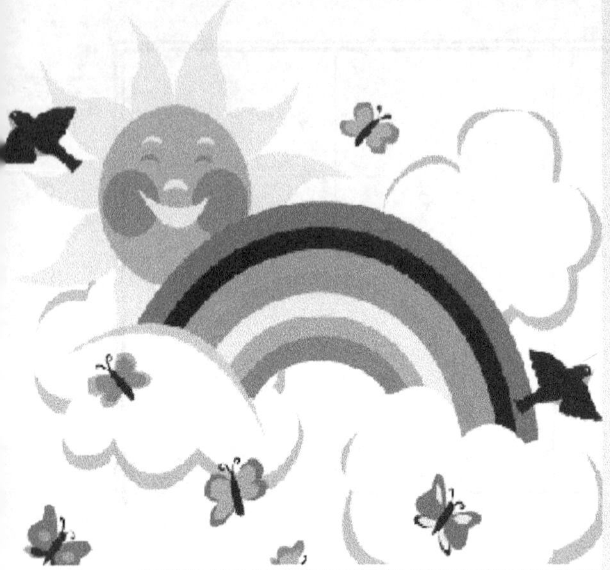

							ك	م	م	ا	ذ	ز	ر	ر	ب	ط
							د	ز	م	ر	ع	خ	و	ر	ح	ش
							و	ش	ل	ث	ل	ل	ض	ص	س	ط
							ح	ض	ص	س	ل	ل	ي	ذ	خ	ت
							ش	ي	ذ	خ	ل	ل	ض	ص	س	ع
							ر	ش	م	ح	ل	ل	ض	س	ش	ض
							د	ص	د	ف	ل	ل	ظ	خ	ح	ش
							م	غ	ع	ت	ل	ل	ت	ث	ب	ي
							ر	ذ	د	ت	ل	ل	ض	ص	ش	ج
							د	ق	ف	ا	ل	ل	ف	م	ع	ش
ر	و	ز	ذ	ط	خ	ج	ح	ب	ذ	م	ل	ل	ف	م	ع	ت
ر	ى	و	د	ر	ي	د	ش	أ	م	ع	ل	ل	ج	ج	ح	ع
د	ز	ي	ر	ل	ل	م	ز	د	خ	ق	ل	ل	ك	ث	ص	ي
د	ق	ز	و	ل	ل	ض	ر	ذ	د	ت	ل	ل	ض	ص	ش	ج
ذ	د	ش	د	ل	ل	ب	د	ق	ف	ا	ل	ل	ف	م	ع	ش
ر	و	ز	ذ	ل	ل	ج	ح	ب	ذ	ل	ل	ل	ف	م	ع	ت
ر	ى	و	د	ل	ل	د	ش	أ	ل	ل	ل	ع	ج	ج	ح	ع
د	ز	ي	ر	د	ل	ل	ل	ل	ل	ل	ع	ف	ك	ث	ص	ي
د	ق	ز	و	ج	ث	ض	ر	ذ	د	ت	ظ	ع	ض	ص	ش	ج
ذ	د	ش	د	ر	ي	ب	د	ق	ف	ا	م	ع	ف	م	ع	ش

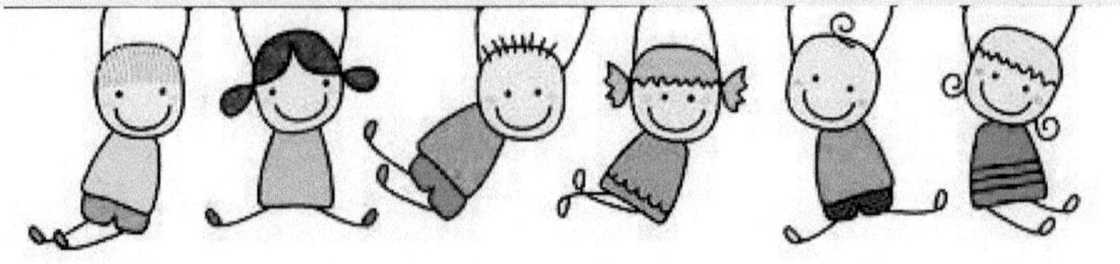

ضع دائرة حول حرف (اللام) (ل) :

Put a circle around the letter (ل):

فلفل
فيل

صل الكلمات التي تبدأ بالحرف (ل) :

Match the letter (ل) to the word that start with it:

- ليمون
- كلب
- ظبي
- لعبة

لون الحرف (ل) :

Color the letter (ل):

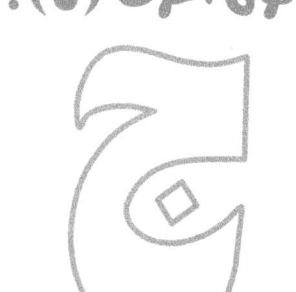 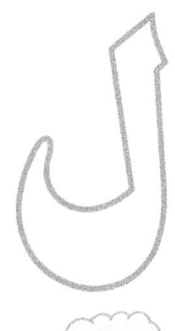 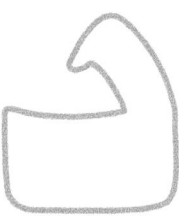

لون الحروف :   Color The letters:

Write the letter that the picture begins with:

لون الحرف الصحيح الذي تبدأ به الكلمات الآتية

Colour in the circle with the correct letter that each word starts with:

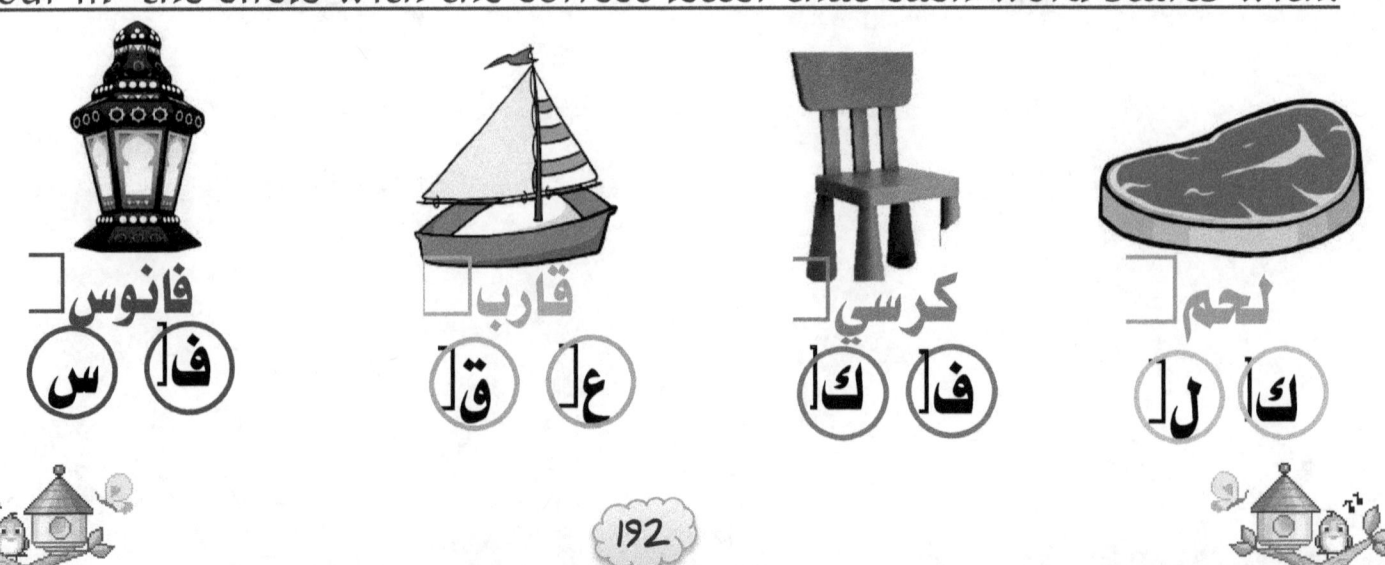

حرف الميم

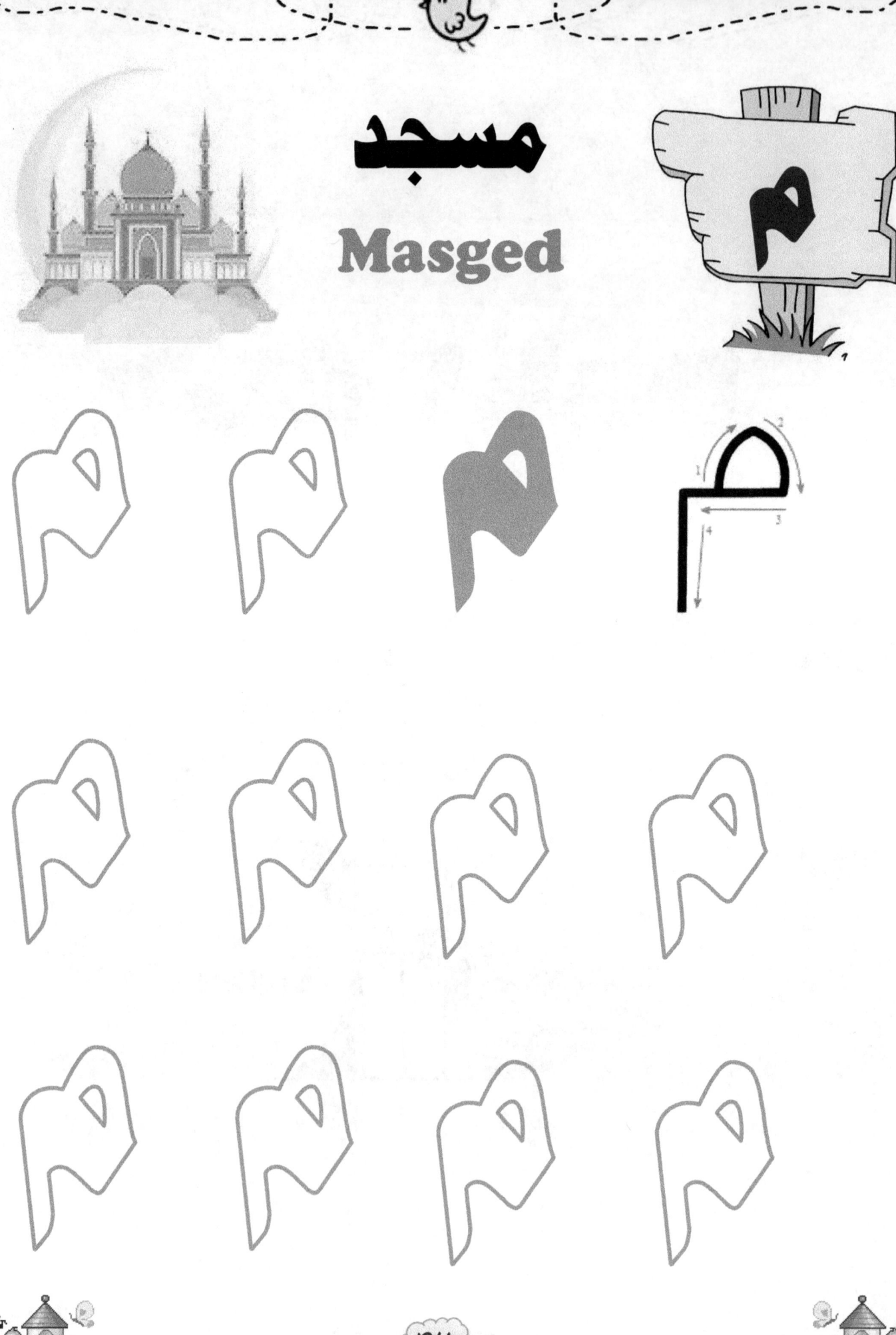

Masged

Trace over the dots:

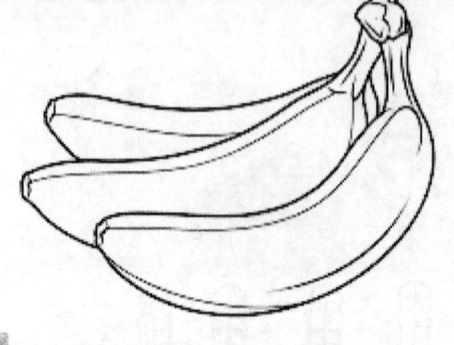

موز
Mooz

Trace over the dots:

ملك

Malek

Trace over the dots:

مفتاح
Moftah

Write letter (م) in each box:

لون المربعات التي تحتوي على الحرف (م):
Color the boxes that have the letter (م):

ضع دائرة حول حرف (الميم) (م):
Put a circle around the letter (م):

قلم   نملة   مفتاح

صل الكلمات التي تبدأ بالحرف (م):
Match the letter (م) to the word that start with it:

ضابط
مفتاح
ثعبان
موز

لون الحرف (م):
Color the letter (م):

حرف النون

نحلة

Nahla

ن

نحلة

Nahla

Trace over the dots:

نمر

Nemr

Trace over the dots:

نجوم
Nogom

Trace over the dots:

نخل
Nakhl

Write letter (ن) in each box:

لون المربعات التي تحتوي على الحرف (ن):
Color the boxes that have the letter (ن):

ضع دائرة حول حرف (النون) (ن):
Put a circle around the letter (ن):

نجوم ☐   منزل ☐   ميزان ☐

صل الكلمات التي تبدأ بالحرف (ن):
Match the letter (ن) to the word that start with it:

لون الحرف (ن):   Color the letter (ن):

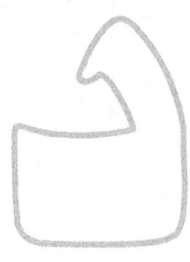

حرف الهاء

هاتف

Hatef

Trace over the dots:

هدهد
Hodod

Trace over the dots:

هلال
Helal

Trace over the dots:

هدية

Hedya

Write letter (ه) in each box:

لون المربعات التي تحتوي على الحرف (هـ):
Color the boxes that have the letter (هـ):

ز	ز	ح	ر	و	خ	ع	ر	م	ز	د	م
ل	ل	خ	ف	ق	ل	ن	خ	ف	ش	و	أ
ت	ت	م	ج	ع	ح	ع	م	ج	ض	ح	ج
د	ش	ي	ك	م	ق	ع	ف	ك			
ش	هـ	هـ	هـ	هـ	هـ	هـ	هـ				
ظ	هـ	هـ	هـ	هـ	هـ	هـ	هـ				
د	هـ	هـ	م	ز	ع	ح	هـ				
ش	هـ	هـ	ر	هـ	هـ	هـ	هـ				
ظ	هـ	ن	هـ	ق	هـ	هـ	هـ				

ت	ح	خ	ف	ق	ل	ن	ذ	ذ	ب	ش	و	ع	م	ن	ق	ر
ج	ج	ح	م	ج	ع	ح	ع	د	أ	ل	م	ج	و	ز	ق	د
ي	ص	م	ك	ف	ع	ق	خ	د	ز	م	ك	د	ر	ي	ز	د

ضع دائرة حول حرف (الهاء) (هـ):
Put a circle around the letter (هـ):

زهرة فهد هلال

صل الكلمات التي تبدأ بالحرف (هـ):
Match the letter (هـ) to the word that start with it:

نملة
هلال
هرم
فيل

هـ

لون الحرف (هـ):
Color the letter (هـ):

حرف الواو

 # وحيد القرن
Wahed- Elqarn

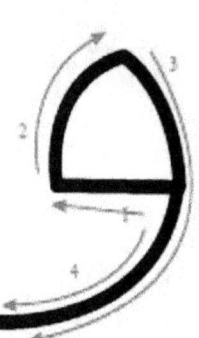   

وحيد القرن
Wahed- Elqarn

Trace over the dots:

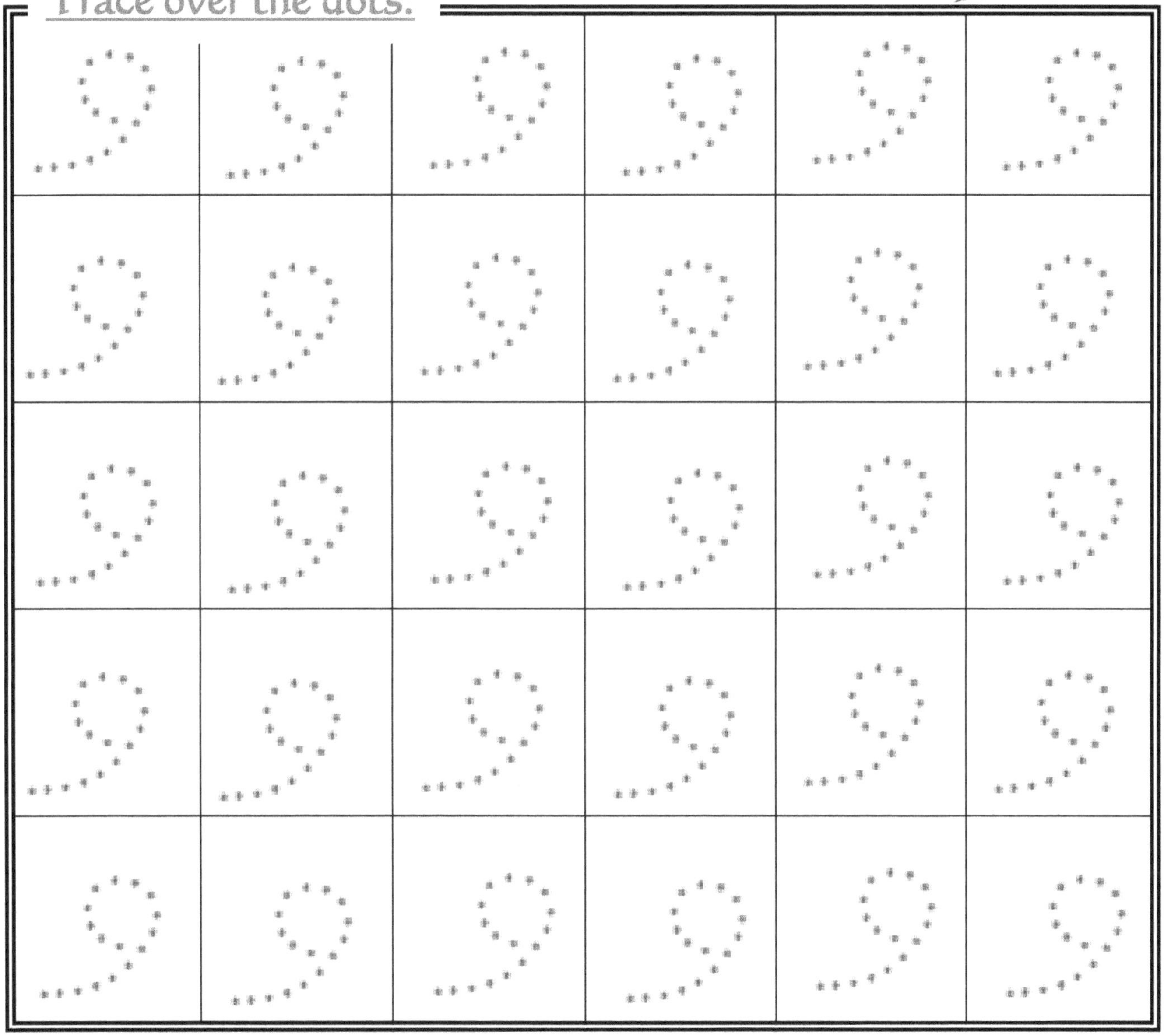

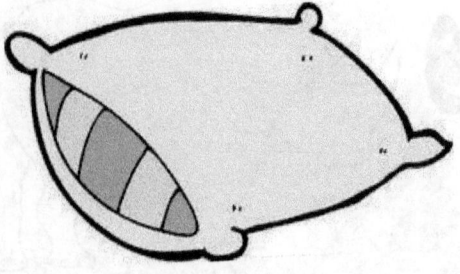
وسادة
Wesada
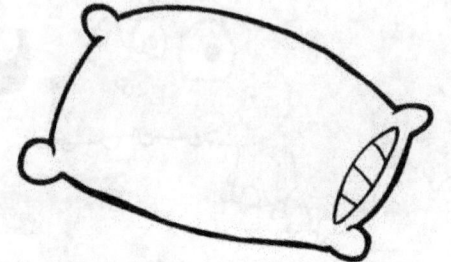

Trace over the dots:

وجه
Wajh

Trace over the dots:

وطواط
Wetwat

Write letter (و) in each box:

لون المربعات التي تحتوي على الحرف (و):
Color the boxes that have the letter (و):

ضع دائرة حول حرف (الواو) (و)

Put a circle around the letter (و):

حلوى ☐   موز ☐   وجه ☐

صل الكلمات التي تبدأ بالحرف (و):

Match the letter (و) to the word that start with it:

هدهد ☐

ولد ☐

شمسية ☐

وحيد القرن ☐

لون الحرف (و):

Color the letter (و):

حرف الياء

ى

يد

Yaad

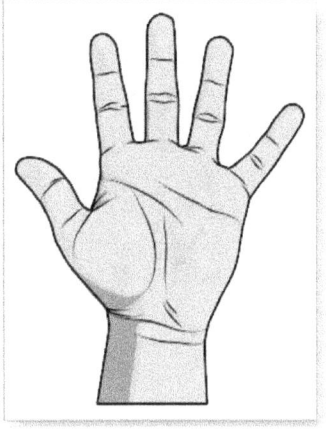 يد

Yaad

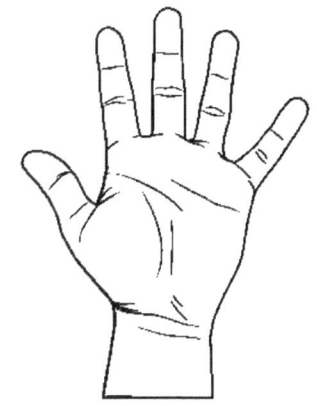

Trace over the dots:

يقطين
Yaqteen

Trace over the dots:

 يخت

Yakht

Trace over the dots:

يرقة
Yaraqa

Write letter (ي) in each box:

لون المربعات التى تحتوى على الحرف (ي) :

Color the boxes that have the letter(ي):

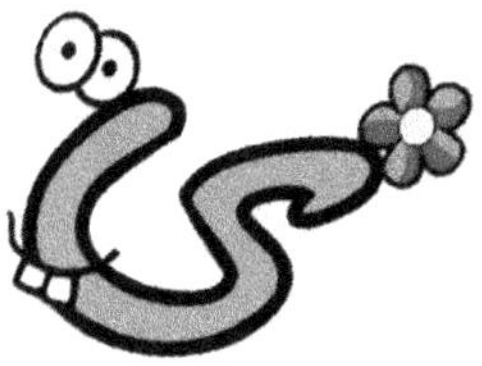

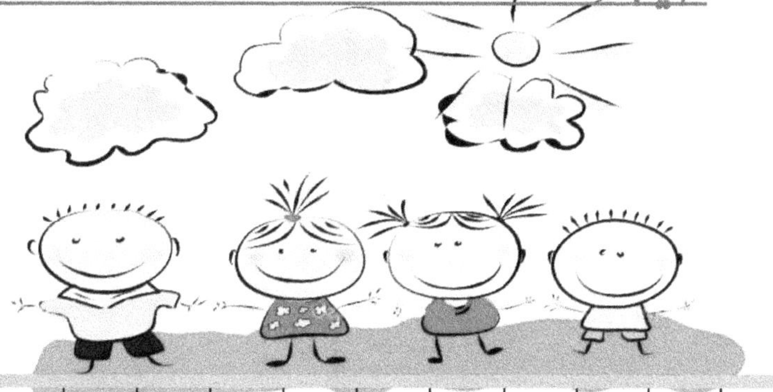

			ن	ن	ك	ق	ف	ت	ظ	ط	ض	ص	ش	خ	ز			
			ط	ظ	خ	ص	ض	ل	ك	ق	ف	غ	ع	ش	ي			
			و	ز	غ	ع	ظ	م	ح	ث	غ	غ	ع	ع	خ			
ع	ث	ر	ى	و	ل	ي	ت	ع	ح	خ	ج	ج	ح	ز	ط	ق	ث	د
			ث	ب	م	ض	ح	ظ	غ	ع	ظ	ح	خ	ص	ض			
			ص	ش	ن	م	ق	ت	ل	ي	ي	ي	ي	ي	ي			
			ي	ي	د	ج	ح	ض	ظ	ي	ي	ي	ي	ي	ي			
			ي	ي	و	ج	ث	ف	ك	ي	ي	ت	ظ	ط	ض			
			ي	ي	د	ر	ي	ض	خ	ي	ي	ل	ك	ق	ف			
			ي	ي	ر	د	ط	ظ	غ	ع	ي	ي	ي	ث	غ			
			ي	ي	م	م	ت	ت	ل	ي	ي	ي	ي	خ	ج			
			ص	ي	ي	ي	ي	ي	ي	ي	ي	ي	ي	ف	ق			
			غ	ع	ي	ي	ي	ي	ي	ي	ي	ي	ي	ي	ت			
			غ	ع	و	ج	ث	ف	ك	ق	ف	ت	ظ	ط	ض			
خ	ع	ج	ج	ح	د	ر	ي	ض	خ	ص	ض	ل	ك	ق	ف	غ	ع	ش
			د	ز	ر	د	ط	ظ	غ	ع	ظ	م	ح	ث	غ			
			ز	م	م	م	ت	ت	ل	ي	ت	ع	ح	خ	ج			
			ز	ي	ر	د	ك	م	ز	د	خ	غ	ع	ف	ق			

ضع دائرة حول حرف (الياء) (ي):

Put a circle around the letter (هـ):

يقطين   تليفون   بيت

صل الكلمات التي تبدأ بالحرف (ي):

Match the letter (ي) to the word that start with it:

Color the letter (ي):   لون الحرف (ي):

حروف
الهجاء

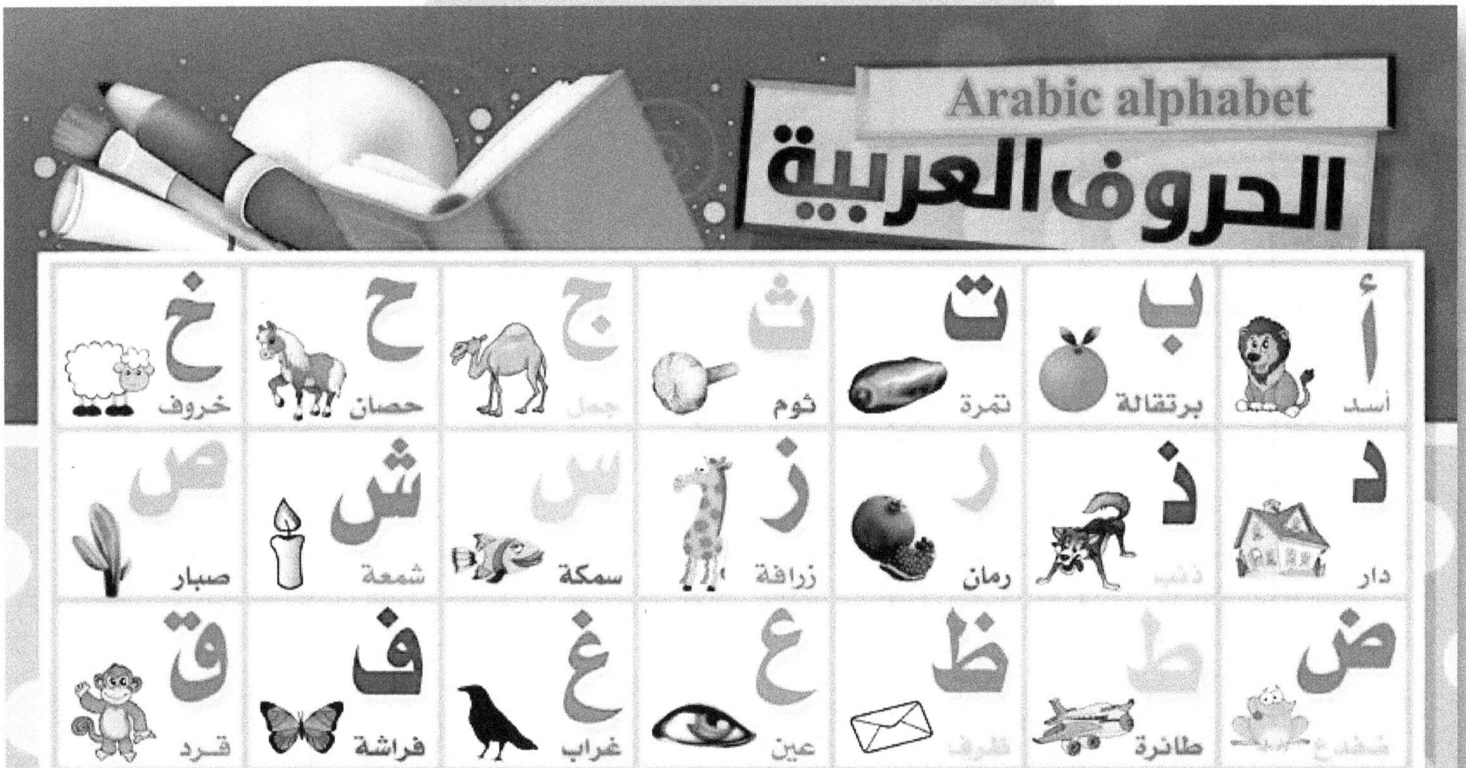
Arabic alphabet
الحروف العربية
أ أسد
ب برتقالة
ت تمرة
ث ثوم
ج جمل
ح حصان
خ خروف
د دار
ذ ذئب
ر رمان
ز زرافة
س سمكة
ش شمعة
ص صبار
ض ضفدع
ط طائرة
ظ ظرف
ع عين
غ غراب
ف فراشة
ق قرد
ك كتاب
ل ليمون
م مسجد
ن نحلة
هـ هاتف
و وردة
ي يد

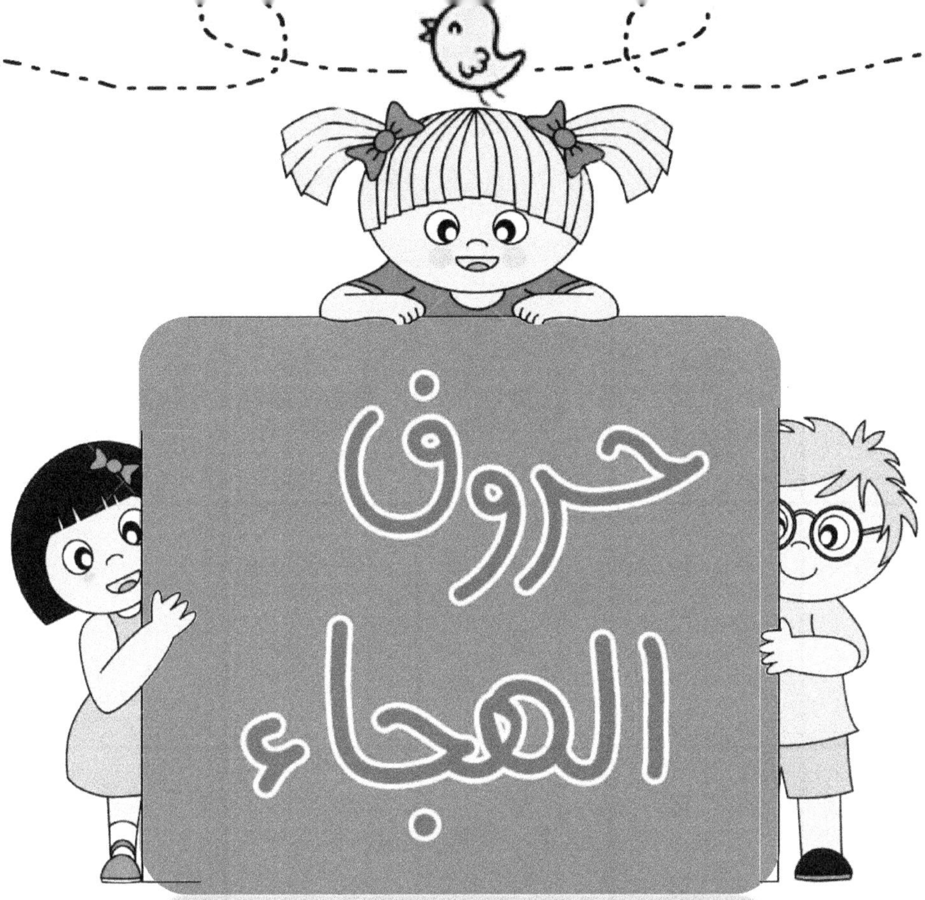

اكتب الحروف الهجائية التالية :

خ	ح	ج	ث	ت	ب	أ

اكتب الحروف الهجائية التالية:

ص	ش	س	ز	ر	ذ	د

اكتب الحروف الهجائية التالية:

ق	ف	غ	ع	ظ	ط	ض

اكتب الحروف الهجائية التالية :

ي	و	هـ	ن	م	ل	ك

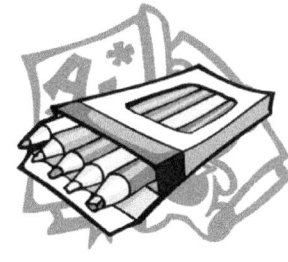

Fill in the missing letter: — أكمل الحرف الناقص ....

 ...ـاج    ...ـطة    ...سد

 ...ـمامة    ...ـمل    ...لعب

 ...راع    ...راجة    ...روف

 ...ـمكة    ...رافة    ...مح

 ...رس    ...ـقر    ...مسية

 ...ـنب    ...ـفر    ...بلة

 ...ـلم    ...ـراولة    ...زال

 ...فتاح    ...ـهبة    ...تاب

 ...قطين    ...جه    ...لال    ...جوم

اكتب الحروف الناقصة في المكان المناسب:

Fill in the missing letters in their proper spots: